A Religion for Our Time

A Religion
for Our Time

Louis Evely

Translated by
Brian and Marie-Claude Thompson

Herder and Herder

1968
HERDER AND HERDER NEW YORK
232 Madison Avenue, New York, N.Y. 10016

Original edition: *Une Religion
pour notre temps,* published by the author.

Nihil obstat: Brendan W. Lawlor, Censor Librorum
Imprimatur: ✝Robert F. Joyce, Bishop of Burlington
. June 7, 1968

Contents

Contents

A Religion for Our Time

I

Poverty of Self

I

Let us start with poverty.

We know that a characteristic of the Christian is that he should be poor. "Blessed are the poor. Blessed are those who hear the word of God," who need something, who are waiting, who are suffering, who are open, who hunger. Happy are the poor, for the kingdom of God is for them. Only the poor man has access to God, because only the poor man goes out of himself and opens himself to God. He is happy who knows that he is poor, for he knows that he is incapable of being happy all by himself.

Poverty is not the crownpiece of Christian life, it is the front door. It is the decisive distinction, from the very beginning, between those who can be Christian and those who cannot. If you are rich, there is nothing to be done with you.

Christ could not do anything with the rich, above all with the rich in religion. The Pharisees were rich, if not with money, at least in their self-sufficiency. They were satisfied with themselves, sure of their knowledge, content in their practices. They knew much better than the Lord what he had to teach them, and they intervened constantly to criticize him. The poor man is he who accepts being called into question by the word of God, who allows himself to be unsettled by God's word, who knows that it is not he who possesses his faith but that it is the faith which possesses him.

To what extent, then, is our faith the true faith? Let us allow ourselves to be criticized by the word of God. Let us allow ourselves to be stripped bare by it. Do you recall that this is its function: to make us poor? "You are already pruned by the word which I have spoken to you" (John 15, 3).

And yet there are people who do not believe in God's word who do us the same service, of calling us into question and making us notice that by dint of preserving it our religion has become a caricature unable to fulfill the expectations of man.

The Second Vatican Council placed the Church anew in a state of poverty. It called into question what had once seemed so self-sufficient. But it is not to so-called "traditional" Catholics that we owe thanks for the renewal now taking place in the Church. *They* were quite content, they wanted nothing to be changed.

Poverty, I have said, is the front door of Christianity. A

good proof of this fact, which each of you has verified, is that as soon as a man becomes somewhat Christian he almost always poses to himself the question of poverty. As soon as he has left the comfortable mediocrity of average Christianity he worries about being rich.

How to be poor is a question which badgers you because at the threshold of genuine religious life you feel that it is this problem in particular which you must solve: "I thank you, Father, for having hidden these things from the wise and understanding and revealed them to infants." This is the decisive point—that which differentiates a Christian from a non-Christian.

What differentiates us from pagans is not necessarily generosity. St. Paul says, "If I give away all I have, and if I deliver my body to be burned, but have not love, I gain nothing." It is possible to be generous without having true charity.

It is poverty which decides: we should not say of a generous, straightforward, honest pagan that "he is a Christian without knowing it." We should wonder if he practices these virtues in poverty, or in superiority, autonomy, self-sufficiency. This is the question: is he a poor man who receives or a rich man who has nothing to give?

It is not enough to admire a virtuous unbeliever; we should try to reveal to him what he lacks: help him to recognize himself as poor. There is no possible conversion unless one experiences poverty.

Julien Green, in his *Journal,* so much more beautiful than

11

his novels, tells about his conversion. Worn out, he says, "I asked that a hand be stretched out to me." Only the poor enter into the kingdom of God. May a hand be stretched out to us . . .

II

What is poverty?

We all know that it is not an economic state. It is not a question of money but a question of heart. The fact of not having money is not a virtue. One can be penniless and have the soul of a rich man. One can also (but it is rare) be a man of property and have the soul of a poor man.

Poverty is a frame of mind and we are all invited to it. It is a certain experience of our human limits which makes us open ourselves to God, and lose our ambition to be self-sufficient. It turns us towards him in expectation and trust.

Every man is a poor man without knowing it, and economic poverty is blessed because it is the sacrament, the sensible sign of a much profounder poverty, —this one universal, the poverty of the soul, the misery of our love and faith. Blessed, I would say, are those who are hungry and thirsty in reality. They are warned, they are initiated, they know that there is something rotten in the kingdom of this world, that they are not made for this world, that they have to turn towards another world.

Poverty and suffering do not always make us better, they do not always bring us closer to *virtue,* but they always bring us closer to *truth.* They tell us about ourselves. Man is poor at the bottom of himself, and if he ceased being poor economically, he would still be terribly poor morally. Material poverty is only a sign, a warning, a symbol of our real poverty.

Each of us should think of how he has experienced the poverty of the world, the limitation of man, the indigence and profound weakness of the human soul.

The burden we bear reveals to each of us what others bear. Our misery is fraternal in the sense that it tells us about the men about us. It is naïve to think that there are people outside of this fraternity, people without need of anyone else. At some level of human experience each man knows that he is poor. At some level of human experience we are all totally insufficient before God.

The apostle is one who has experienced misery of this kind, who has accepted his poverty before God because he has found something to sustain him in his misfortune, something strong enough to bear his weakness, and who is then able to go to the others and invite each of them to accept his own poverty as he has accepted his.

Thus the apostle must go to the others with the face of a poor man. What characterizes him is the profound experience he has of his nullity and of the great things God can do in the poverty of his servant. And he goes to the others in this attitude of respect, of total welcome, which allows each one to open up to his own poverty before him.

The apostle goes about the world as one who is vulnerable, poor, and weak, but he is confident also that there is no greater strength than daring to be weak in this way.

III

In order to love anyone, no less than a miracle is necessary: the invasion of the whole love of God into your heart so that you will be able to meet this demand. This is what a theological virtue is: a force which comes from God. For you to be able to have a little faith, a little true hope, a little true love, a miracle is necessary; something super-natural—you have to open yourself to God. There is no faith unless doubt has been overcome, there is no hope unless despair has been surmounted, and there is no true love unless indifference or hate has been vanquished.

We who live the theological virtues are poor because we know that no less than a force of God in our heart is necessary for us to be able to love someone truly and faithfully. We are by ourselves sterile in love, sterile in faith, sterile in hope, and this is true human poverty.

IV

Here are some questions, both large and small, which are raised by the problem of poverty.

"Is not the faith which makes us strong also a kind of richness?"

No. Faith is faith in Another, in what he does in our poverty. The more you have faith in God, the more you have the feeling of your smallness. No one has ever known God without knowing himself to be poor and a sinner. St. Paul himself asked that faith, in him, be transformed into richness: ". . . a thorn was given me in the flesh, a messenger of Satan, to harass me, to keep me from being too elated. Three times I besought the Lord about this, that it should leave me; but he said to me, 'My grace is sufficient for you, for my power is made perfect in weakness'" (2 Corinthians 12, 7–9).

In the same way, hope is not a richness. You hope in God and not in your own hope. You hope in him whom you address, not in what you ask him for.

"But if I am constantly to call into question my hope, how will I be able to communicate it to others?"

You should place a total confidence and hope in God, but not in the ways and means in which you imagine it will be realized. *Spes contra spes,* to hope in spite of all hope. Christ himself began by asking God for the wrong thing. God disappoints our wishes in order to open us to his hope. We must always pray and hope in God. But we will be heard in a way different from what we had thought. Christ asked, "If it be possible, let this cup pass from me . . ." (Matthew 26, 39), and he was heard in receiving the strength to drink it. His wish was disappointed but not his hope.

"In the days of his flesh, Jesus offered up prayers and supplications, with loud cries and tears, to him who was able to save him from death, and he was heard for his godly fear. Although he was a Son, he learned obedience through what he suffered . . ." (Hebrews 5, 7–8).

This is how we are heard. He asked to be set free from death: he was heard, he received the strength to bear it.

For faith, it is the same: "I have total faith in God." This means: "I am sure of having met him. I know very well that he has acted around me and in me. I am sure of it, but I always call into question the forms of my faith. Have I really understood, I ask myself. Shouldn't I understand better?" We unceasingly learn the object of our faith.

"How do I know that God is living? How do I know that he is love? How do I know that he is a person and not an idea?"

This is an immense question, one which our entire book tries to answer. But here is the schema.

First stage: availability and openness are necessary before

anything else. If you want to go from agnosticism to true religion, you must begin by putting yourself in a disposition of poverty; you must experience your need of God, and know that his truth is someone and not something. Ask for a hand to be stretched out to you. You should not invent God, you should pray to him to reveal himself to you. One does not conquer God. He gives himself and he reveals himself as he wants. "I am the handmaid of the Lord" (Luke 1, 38). This is the indispensable disposition.

Second stage: there is the question of proofs. It is the most dangerous. There are good proofs of the existence of God, but they can lead the unbeliever in a rationalistic direction.

Third stage: this is the stage of faith. God exists and has spoken to me. Read the Gospel. "My sheep hear my voice and follow me." "Their hearts burnt within them while he opened to them the Scriptures." Impulses of infinite joy, liberation, and peace burst forth in their hearts. They knew that God alone could speak in this way, that God alone could love in this way, that God alone could forgive in this way. Read the whole Gospel. It is on this word that one makes up one's mind for or against Christ, on a certain impression he has made on the heart, and it is overwhelming— it is overwhelming to have to decide.

"Then you decide on the basis of your impressions. Your faith is based only upon your feelings!"

In what will you recognize God if not in the fact that he

17

is like no one else, in the fact that he reaches us at a depth where no one else has ever touched us?

But here is my apologetics better formulated:

There is an inner fact, which is in man, and an exterior fact, which is the Church. These two facts meet and confirm each other. I believe in the inner fact (reading of the Gospel, prayer, celebration of a sacrament, encounter with a person or an event, and the impression they have made on me), but I dare to believe in it totally only because it is confirmed, announced, described, certified in an exterior fact (the Church, its doctrine, its history).

Inversely, I believe in the Church, in all that it teaches me, because inwardly I have what is necessary to understand what it says to me, to put contents into its dogmas and a life beneath the forms it prescribes to me.

I would not believe in my impressions if I did not believe in the Church, but I would not believe in the Church if I did not encounter in it the impression of God.

The Church gives me this precious assurance: that what I believe with all my heart is not merely subjective historical fact, continued through centuries by the Church.

God has spoken to each of us on one occasion or another, and all the difference between a saint and ourselves is that the saints are attentive to receive and preserve the impressions which God has made on their hearts. They are faithful and we are not. It is here that man's freedom expresses itself in relation to God: our prodigious capacity to forget. If you were to witness the most striking miracle, a year later it would be as difficult for you to believe in the miracle as to believe in God. It is as easy to call this miracle into question as to call into question any impression of God in prayer, in a sacrament, in a reading of the Gospel. Between God and us almost the same thing happens as between us and very dear friends whom we knew when we were young. Do you not remember them? You used to spend vacation with them all the time, you had never met such a friendly family, and then, you do not really know why, relations became more infrequent, you began to make other acquaintances, though on the whole they were much less dear than the former. You will never love anyone as you loved those early friends, and nonetheless, it is terrible to say, at the proposition of seeing them again you feel uneasy. You prefer to remain as you are. It is too difficult to change.

Between God and us it is very often the same thing. There have been strong impressions of God in our life, there have been revelations. Our God is a God who reveals himself, he is the God of revelation, the God who speaks, the God who moves and acts, the God who "enlightens every man," the God who makes himself recognized. But what is terrible is that after having recognized him, we can completely lose touch with him, remembering the time when we knew him so well, and no longer having the courage to start all over again doing what is necessary to get in touch with him again.

This is man's freedom. Everything depends on freedom in the domain of religion.

This God speaks, he reveals himself: in the true celebration of a sacrament, a true prayer, a true attention to your life, a true attention to others. In the ancient Church, when it was necessary to choose a man for a mission, one chose someone really full of the Holy Spirit. I can assure you that one could see it. Have you not met someone really full of the Holy Spirit? Peter asserts in his address after Pentecost, "Having received from the Father the promise of the Holy Spirit, he has poured out this which you see and hear" (Acts 2, 33). Do you feel that you have seen and heard the Holy Spirit? One *experiences* God. I could very easily write a biography of the Holy Spirit in your life. For example, how is it that, in spite of everything, you are taking the time to read this book? It is through the action of the Holy Spirit. And at bottom, you do not doubt it. And you are poor, you have come to do it a little in spite of yourself, so powerful is the Holy Spirit. He bites and bites again, the Holy Spirit. It is above all when one interferes with him that one feels him, and one feels him more and more as one grows older.

Let us consider the vocation of St. Peter.

"Peter, when you were young, you were full of illusions, you went where you liked, you did what you liked, but when you are older, Peter, another will take you by the hand and lead you where you did not want to go." This is the poor man, he is led beyond his wish, but to the place of his hope. This is the experience of God in your life. The Holy Spirit acts and murmurs . . . I am going to tell you something I have just learned: fortunately, the Holy Spirit is not a dove. This image is absolutely discouraging. I have learned that the image of a dove was chosen not because of the shape of the bird, but because of the moan. The dove murmurs all the time. It is because the Holy Spirit moans all the time that he is represented under the form of a dove; it is a verbal and not a plastic image. "The Spirit helps us in our weakness, for we do not know how to pray as we ought, but the Spirit himself intercedes for us with sighs too deep for words" (Romans 8, 26).

V

Let us go deeper into the notion of poverty, for it is fundamental. It is very well to say, "I am a sinner, I am poor, I am weak." But these words will tempt no one, they will not convert anyone.

The poor man is he who for the *love* of God accepts his poverty, who knows God enough to accept to be poor before him. There is no greater strength than to dare to be weak in this way. The man who is able to bear his poverty, his weakness, is not bitter or desperate or discouraged. On the contrary, he believes in the great things which God will do in the poverty of his servant. The man who does not vacillate either in the greatness of his hope, or in the reality of his misery, is a strong man. He is a complete man, well-balanced and happy. He will never break. Whereas a Stoic is a fellow with a cramp. He stiffens, takes up poses, he hardens. But the Christian knows that all the tragedy in the world is true, and that nonetheless life will turn out well. The man who knows he is weak before God is strong in God. The man who knows himself to be poor before God is rich in God—not in himself, but in God. He can welcome everything. He is in harmony with all that is real. The only true man is the poor man.

VI

We have understood nothing about poverty if we have not understood that its source is in God. God is poor. Poverty is a theological virtue. The beatitudes are the confidential revelation of the ways of God. Hear all of the beatitudes in this way. Jesus confided to us the secret of the way in which he truly lives. He is poor. He places all of his satisfaction in another, he has nothing that he does not want to give to the Father. The Son has nothing by himself. He does nothing on his own, but only what he sees the Father do. "The words that I say to you I do not speak on my own authority; but the Father who dwells in me does his works" (John 14, 10). Whoever sees Jesus sees the Father. And the Holy Spirit does not speak on his own: "Whatever he hears, he will speak" (John 16, 13); "he will bear witness to me" (John 15, 26).

God is poor, God makes way for another. God places all

his richness in another. He is total gift of himself. What kind of idea do you have of God? This is the whole problem. Among all the influences which combine to give a direction to your life, there is none more important than the idea you have of God. The whole history of mankind has been distorted because Adam had a false idea of God. Adam wanted to become like God. But what does that mean?

"Be perfect even as your heavenly Father is perfect." This was not Adam's sin. If he had truly wanted to become like God, what luck! Unfortunately, he had a false idea of God: he thought God was rich, autonomous, self-sufficient, precisely not poor. And so in order to become unlike God, he disobeyed, he set himself free, he became independent.

We should be careful, for we will each become like the God we imagine him to be. If we imagine him as rich, solitary, powerful, autonomous, self-sufficient, invulnerable, we will strive to become like that image. But if we know the true God, then we will strive to love others more, to grow in solidarity with them, to become more attached and attentive to them, more obedient to their wishes. We will welcome them always, and be their servant.

VII

Poverty implies a threefold relation: to God, to goods, and to others. Let us describe this last one now.

The best definition of poverty which I have heard is this:

"The poor man is someone in whose home everyone feels at ease."

There is no question here of making your home as shabby as possible: that would discourage others from coming! It should simply be beautiful enough, comfortable enough, welcoming enough for everybody to enjoy it and unfold in it. Above all, let it be "open."

The poor man knows how to receive.

To give is often the act of the rich man: one gives from above to below. But to receive is the act of the poor man.

What Christ reproaches money for is that it divides men. The man who is attached to money shatters the work of God: human community. He violates the two great commandments of God: he recognizes neither God as a Father, nor man as a brother.

Woe to the rich man: he cuts himself off from God, because he places his confidence elsewhere. And he cuts himself off from his brothers because he ignores them, exploits them, sets them aside, because he prefers his gold to their company.

Poverty makes us fraternal; but the rich man is a solitary person. He must isolate himself in order to defend his riches. If he had been generous he would not have become rich. He must keep the poor at a distance always.

In the parable of Lazarus, what is the rich man reproached for? He did not acquire his goods in an illegitimate way, nor did he take advantage of Lazarus's poverty in order to exploit him by employing him for tasks which nobody else wanted to do. What wrong did the rich man do? He did not see Lazarus, that was all. Well, he will not see him for all eternity. It is terrible. The distance which he set between himself and the poor man is a distance which he set between himself and God, for the kingdom of God is for the poor, and he who breaks off with the poor man breaks off with God. It is terrible. It is frightening. One thinks one is deciding only in relation to men and one is deciding in relation to God. It makes one quiver. He did nothing positively bad, the rich man; he did not see Lazarus, and he will never see him again.

VIII

Poverty is, finally, a certain behavior towards goods.

It is not trading in an expensive automobile for a stripped-down economy compact. An acquired poverty is a contradiction in terms. Poverty is one of those surprising virtues, like humility: as soon as you believe you have it, you no longer do.

I do not recommend a "medieval" type of poverty: distributing all your goods to the poor, getting rid, all of a sudden, of your wealth and putting its burden on the shoulders of others. I believe that it is far preferable for you to learn how to make good use of what you now have.

Your essential duty is to invent the poverty of our time, the type of poverty which suits it; nothing is more indispensable in a technical civilization. A wise use of your goods will be infinitely more beneficial than a total renunciation of them.

IX

Do not spend money inconsiderately, but do not save it simply in the belief that you are practicing virtue. Spend it usefully. Before any purchase, ask yourself if others will benefit from it, if they will be more at ease in your home. You will never do enough of that.

A better piece of advice: do not try to impoverish yourself. Do not torment yourself by snatching your goods out of your own hands. Poverty seldom leads to love. But genuine love always leads to poverty.

A few years ago, when the Lenten fast was mandatory, did you think you were pleasing God by depriving yourself of steak . . . and treating yourself to a delicious fish?

Your "mortification" will please God only if it benefits others. It will thus benefit yourself infinitely more as well. You do not need "mortification," but "vivification." Vivify others and yourselves through a true charity.

What God asks from you is to love one another, and not to torture yourself solitarily. Do not rack your brain for ways of depriving yourself, do not embitter yourself by gratuitous mortifications. Love others and you will soon be poor.

The story is told of two zealous young converts in Africa who had taken the habit of putting themselves, with their car, at the disposal of people for driving them to or picking them up at the railway station. Well, after a very short while, people would call them from the station, saying, "Come at once to get us!" And if they happened sometimes to excuse themselves: "We are not free. Please wait for an hour . . . ," they would get a bawling out.

Know that if you begin, if you open your home, you will become poor very quickly; you will no longer have anything of your own. People will manage beautifully to cultivate your poverty.

Your mortifications, your impoverishments, your crosses should not come from your own personal workshop. Let the others furnish them to you. Quality is guaranteed!

Happy the poor man, for he is dispensed from being rich. He lives in joint possession with providence. He accepts a certain necessary insecurity, because he has a Father in heaven and brothers on earth.

Happy the poor man, for he is filial, free, fraternal. He has entered the kingdom of God. He has begun to enjoy a life and a happiness which belong to him forever.

II

The Incarnate Fullness

I

We cannot be Christian unless we believe in the salvation of the world. We love a God who loves the world, who did everything in order to save the world, and who, every day, sends his son (this is you), his only beloved daughter, in whom he is well pleased (this is you), into the world to save it. This is your morning prayer.

A Hindu sage has said that Christians have so far understood half of Christianity. They have understood that God and Christ are the same thing. But they have not yet understood that Christ and man are the same thing. That Christ is still man now and is in every man. That the Incarnation of Christ in a particular human nature had but preceded and earned his Incarnation, let us say his penetration, his "solidarization" with all humanity. There is no man untouched by the Incarnation of Christ, by the influence of Christ. He

29

"enlightens every man who comes into the world." In every man God lives and waits to be discerned in order to grow in him. This is your Christian faith. God lives in every man and we look for him in the clouds. There is a passage from St. Luke which should make us all rejoice. It concerns an apparition to the disciples, in Jerusalem: "As they were saying this, Jesus himself stood among them. But they were startled and frightened, and supposed that they saw a spirit. And he said to them, 'Why are you troubled, and why do questionings rise in your hearts? See my hands and my feet, that it is I, myself; handle me, and see; for a spirit has not flesh and bones as you see that I have.' And while they still disbelieved for joy, and wondered, he said to them, 'Have you anything here to eat?' They gave him a piece of broiled fish, and he took it and ate before them" (Luke 24, 36–43).

The apostles have an apparition of the risen Christ. They think they see a ghost, a spirit, they are afraid. Christ reassures them and says, "Look, I am real, with flesh and bones. And you don't believe yet? Well, come on, we're going to have a bite to eat and something to drink."

The difference with modern Christians is that they would be delighted if Christ *were* only a spirit. But when they are told, "Christ is your neighbor," they say, "Oh, how pedestrian. *I* have religious exaltations, I pray, I go to the chapel, I have good relations with God, but let's not mix up everything in the same pot."

The true religion is that *Jesus* has flesh and bones, that he is incarnate. John says so twice, in his first epistle (4, 2), and again in his second (verse 7). "By this you know the Spirit of God; every spirit which confesses that Jesus Christ has come in the flesh is of God, and every spirit which does not confess Jesus is not of God."

For you, is Jesus incarnate? Is he living, in the midst of you, in the flesh? Or is he a spirit, a ghost? We are going to go deeper into this question.

All the newness of Christianity lies in the new commandment of Christ. What is this new commandment? The answer is not "Love one another, and love your neighbor as yourself." For I then reply "This was already in the Old Testament, it is nothing new." For the answer let us turn to Matthew.

"When the Pharisees heard that he had silenced the Sadducees, they came together. And one of them, a lawyer, asked him a question to test him. 'Teacher, which is the great commandment in the law?' And he said to him, 'You shall love the Lord your God with all your heart, and with all your soul, and with all your mind. This is the great and first commandment. And a second is like it, You shall love your neighbor as yourself' " (22, 34–39).

Do you know where all the newness is? In the little word "like." The second commandment has become like the first. Since when? Since the Incarnation, because God became man. These two commandments have become the same. You find God in your neighbor. Your true religion is measured now, not by the number of your communions, but by your attitude towards your neighbor.

31

An ancient agraphon—that is, a saying not found in the Gospel but thought to have been one of Christ's—says, "Lift up the stone, I am there; split the wood, there I am; you see your brother, you see your God."

St. John records these words: "If any one says, 'I love God,' and hates his brother, he is a liar; for he who does not love his brother whom he has seen, cannot love God whom he has not seen" (1 John 4, 20).

It is not always easy to love your neighbor, but the real difficulty is in loving the reality of the Incarnation. In the history of the Church, all of the heresies aim at the Incarnation, they aim at getting rid of this unbearable thing: that God became man.

II

There is only one proof that Christ is alive: his love is alive in the world, and it makes people do things which nothing human could.

If I believe in the Church and if I believe in God, it is because I have seen his love alive in the world, in people whom I have met. In them, I have met the Church. It is rare to meet the true Church. Many of my old students lost their faith: they had never met the Church. They had never had a motive for faith in proportion to their needs. What is the Church? What had they seen in the churches? A group of people completely indifferent to one another, each pretending to put himself right with God, to be quits with him! But they had never met the true Church. What is the true Church? A group of adults who love one another, a group of adults different enough from one another for their reciprocal understanding, trust, and love to be a miracle. Have you ever met someone who loved in a humanly inexplicable way? If you have, you know that Christ is alive in the world, because his love lives in the world, and that is proof of the Resurrection of Christ.

The world will have faith only if we give it the impression of God, only if it sees Christ alive in the charity of his members, "When two or three are gathered, together in my name, I am among them." When the members of Christ are gathered together, Christ is there. He has once more a body. There too there is exposition of the holy sacrament. But most of the time the members of Christ are not gathered together. They are side by side but there is no organic link among them. They are like pieces of a watch which have been strewn upon a table. If only they could be truly assembled.

But if the church-body came alive again through the reunification of its members, if it could be seen, it is the sight which would convert the world. The only face which Christ can show to our contemporaries in order to convert them is that of our fraternal communities: "See how they love one another."

The world of today will never convert to God if it does not convert to a true Church. After all, the world has this advantage: it is realistic, it will not believe in "proofs," it does not believe in "reasons." It is distrustful, it does not believe in ideas, it has been deceived too often. Everything has been stated, proved, and refuted. So the world is like Thomas: it wants to see and touch the flesh and the bone. It needs a true Church, then it will believe in God. It will not believe in God before believing in a true Church. It wants visible proof that God is alive in the world and it can have only one: that his love is living in the world. That you do things which are beyond yourselves, that *his* love is living in you, that you are poor men in whom he does great things.

And what is the hardest to do, is to love one another. This is what the world stumbles against. This is what it cannot do, this is the miracle, at the level of contemporary interest. You will not truly have faith, and you will even lose your faith, if you do not find people who love one another in this way. Your faith fluctuates exactly according to these encounters. That is why your predication is so important. If you love one another, you show Christ.

In this time of aggiornamento we are going to love one another more closely in the Church. All of the reforms will have to be carried out in an atmosphere of great love, for if no current of extraordinary charity goes through them, they will result only in cruel disappointments, divisions, and rancor within the Church.

The essential would be a Spirit of love, but then it will be a miracle, it will be a pentecost so much stronger than the first one: that beings of all races, of all continents, of all colors, succeed in taking together the common responsibility of the Church and in loving one another enough to get along.

St. John, who has such a sacramental Gospel, is the only one not to report the institution of the Eucharist. Do you know what he replaces it with? With the washing of feet. If you read this passage you will see that it begins like the Mass, with a kind of preface.

"Now before the feast of the Passover, when Jesus knew that his hour had come to depart out of this world to the Father, having loved his own who were in the world, he loved them to the end. And during supper, when the devil had already put into the heart of Judas Iscariot, Simon's son, to betray him, Jesus, knowing that the Father had given all things into his hands, and that he had come from God and was going to God, rose from supper, laid aside his garments, and girded himself with a towel" (13, 1-5).

One passes from celestial religion to incarnate religion: "he girded himself with a towel." And it ends up exactly like a consecration: "As often as you shall do these things, you shall do them in memory of me." "I have given you an example, that you also should do as I have done to you."

So what does it mean? You can be dispensed from all of the sacraments. You can replace baptism in water by baptism of desire or of blood. You can replace real communion by spiritual communion. You can replace confession by a perfect act of contrition. But there is one sacrament, one presence of Christ, which is irreplaceable. There is one sacrament which does not have any substitute, and it is the love of one's neighbor. To be sure, you will not be able to go to communion every morning. You will not be able to go to confession every week in the situations in which you will be. But there will be one sacrament, one presence of Christ, through and in which you will always be able to unite: a humble service given to your neighbor. Within your reach, there is a sacrament, a presence of God which you can always venerate.

III

We Must Become Like God

I

At the beginning of this book we said that the true religion is the religion of the poor man, the genuine apostle is the poor man. We Christians are not better than others, but our religion is better than the others. Our God is better than the other gods.

The apologetic argument in regard to other religions is to say: you are right in being religious, you are right to adore God, to love him, to want to draw closer to him. But you are much more right than you think: because God is much better than you thought. *He* took all the steps to meet you which you imagine you are taking to meet him. *He* is the one who has moved. *He* loves you even when you do not love him. *He* calls you. The hunger which man has for God is nothing in comparison with the hunger which God has for man. Man can be without God, man can attempt to do without God, but God cannot do without man, since he became man-God. A son can deny his father, but a father cannot deny his son. "Even if a mother were to forget her child, *I* will not forget you," the Lord says.

We must correct Pascal: "You would not seek me, if you had not already found me." This is true, but it is not yet true enough. Rather: "You would not seek me, if I had not already found you."

If you are seeking, it is because he has found you, it is because he has begun. If you happen to go somewhere and pray, you should burst with joy, saying: "God is so alive in me that he has already led me this far." And God knows how many obstacles had to be overcome! Then if you sit down and stay long enough, you are finally going to know what he wanted to tell you, what he wanted to give you. To pray is to put yourself at the disposal of God for him to be able once to do in us what he wants to do all the time. For him to be able to say once what he wants to tell us all the time and what we never leave him the time, the leisure, to say. God needs time, a great deal of time, because he has much to tell us and much to do in us.

Our God is better than the others: he is the God-man. He is the God who loves men. He is the God who is much more human than any one among us. He is the Incarnate One.

Our religion of poverty is also the only realistic one. *We* reckon with sin, we are the only ones in the world to reckon with our sin, our total misery, and we are not discouraged by it. We have enough confidence in God to have a minimum of confidence in ourself. He is capable of doing things with the poverty of his servant. We are strong enough to bear our weakness. It is indeed a great deal to be strong enough to bear one's own weakness. There is no greater strength than to dare to be poor, no greater strength than to bear one's misery, one's obscurity, smallness, infirmity, and to believe enough in God to be well-balanced, happy, screne, glad, free of oneself. Not overburdened by one's miseries. The Christian is not someone who believes in sin, he is someone who believes in the forgiveness of sins, which is completely different. He believes that there is a force of salvation in the world, that there is a force which forgives sin in the world. He has been forgiven, washed, purified, cleared of all the evil he has done. Have you had this experience?

To confess your sins is to experience the force of the Resurrection in the world. You will die to your desires which are your sins, and you will be resurrected to the will of God which is love, patience, confidence, tenderness, openness, indulgence, joy.

II

Where and when did you become aware of our awful lack of fraternity?

I did for the first time at the end of the "great war." I saw in 1918, in Brussels, in its streets, cafés, and tramways, thousands of men in uniform, of every creed, every language, every country. They called joyously to one another, joked with one another, shared cigarettes, had drinks together. And I, a child, already paralyzed by shyness and social conventions, discovered with stupefaction, fear, and envy what a fraternal world was.

Alas! a few weeks later it was all over, everything was "in order" again—everyone had again become a civilian, a notary public, a worker, an engineer, a businessman. Everyone was isolated again, shut up in his own categories, stiff with prejudices, arrogant with superiority, or with his resentment for his inferiority.

I found fraternity again in 1940. The first effect of the bombings was to break down barriers in people's hearts. Each compatriot was a wounded person whom we would have liked to soothe. We had never felt so much affection for one another in peace. We felt treasures of generosity, sympathy, fraternity in misfortune.

It is terrible to say, but for me war was the time when we really loved one another!

Who will make us know a peace which does not make us long for war?

III

Why is our religion essentially a religion of community?

Because God is community! And because we must become like him, "perfect, as the Father is perfect."

God had to be more than one to be God. If God were solitary, he would not be God. He is God only because he is Father. He is God only because he is Son. He is God only because he is love exchanged, and this is the Holy Spirit.

Do you know what it means: to need others in order to be yourself? Are you more yourself in isolation? Do you relish "all the dark pleasures of a melancholy heart," or are you happy in a fraternal collaboration and sharing?

When you were a child you resembled God in this: you needed your parents in order to be yourself. "The Son can do nothing by himself." A child who has momentarily lost his parents is said to be lost. He will find himself again, he will once more become peaceful, happy, tender, kind, and generous, only in the arms of his mother. He needs others in order to be himself.

He who loves enters into a certain experience of God. He has found a person with whom he dares to show himself humble, tender, kind, disarmed, vulnerable, as he has never been able to be with anybody else.

A true wife needs her husband in order to be herself. Without him, she is lost, she hesitates, she has no taste for anything, she does not know what she wants (oh! when he is there, she knows very well . . . and it is usually something completely different from what he wants. But he has to be there for her to know!). And a husband without his wife is helpless, diminished; he goes back to the mediocrity, to the carelessness of the bachelor.

Do you have genuine friends? Have you had the joy of working in a genuine community? A community is this:

a milieu in which one is so much more oneself thanks to the others. In which the confidence, the friendship of others, the example and the generosity of others reveal you to yourself, make you capable of giving yourself, of devoting yourself as you never thought you would be able to do.

Do you understand now the preface of the Holy Trinity? For what do we congratulate God? For what do we give him thanks? For what do we rejoice? "Ah! it is truly right and just, proper and helpful towards salvation, that we always and everywhere give thanks to you" because you exist "not in the unity of a single person but in the Trinity of one substance." Not in the isolation, selfishness, narrowness of a single person, but in the sharing of one and the same substance.

You say to God: "What a blessing that you are more than one! What a blessing that you are not solitary, what a blessing that you are not an individualist! What a blessing that you are Father! What a blessing that you are the most beautiful and the most encouraging image of what I am to become!"

For we are all called to become father and mother, that is to say, to arouse life, growth, and joy around us. To engender to the life of the body is little. How many children are born orphans? They have been given a physical life and they are refused all the others. All men are orphans who seek him or her who will awaken them to true life, to faith, friendship, confidence, hope, joy.

Thus we are all father and mother: what do you awaken

around you? A little life? a little affection? a little faith? a little joy? Or only envy, resentment, desire?

If you want to become like God, then, become a father, become a mother. You have no other career, no other religion.

When God wanted to create man like himself, he created him more than one, needing another in order to be himself. He created him capable of loving, inapt at being self-sufficient, at satisfying himself, at withdrawing into himself. Man was made to give himself, to find in another his complement, to be pleased in another. Made for preferring himself in another rather than in himself, made for understanding himself better, appreciating himself better in the image of his own nature revealed to him by another being who relieves him of himself, of his selfishness, of his solitude.

God is like this. The Father does know himself well, does not love himself. He knows himself, loves himself really only in his Son, in whom he is well pleased.

So he made us like him, capable of doing more for the others than we would do for ourselves. If it were only a matter of ourselves we would still put up with our mediocrity. But how can we accept to transmit it to someone else? Your faith awakens when you bring it to others.

For the others you want to have faith, for your children, for your neighbors. For the others you feel that you cannot remain so inconsistent, so weak. You are in the image of God: you need the others in order to be yourself. You can do more for another than you could do for yourself. And if you go to the limit of yourself, you will find yourself more easily in another to whom you have given everything. And all that you have kept for yourself is waste. All that you have not handed down to your children, all that you have not communicated of yourself, is awful, is lost. This is how you are in the image of God: in your capacity to love.

"Outside of the Church, no salvation"—to me this means: outside of a Church, of a Communion, of a community, there is no salvation. Outside of charity, no salvation. That is why the Lord gave us a sacrament without substitute: your neighbor's feet to wash, his shoes to polish. It is impossible for you to be deprived of that. God could not leave you without a sacrament, without an authentic presence of the sacred. So he gave you the washing of feet which surpasses all the sacraments, since all the sacraments can have substitutes, but not your neighbor: you always have *him* within reach.

IV

"What to me is the multitude of your sacrifices? says the Lord; I have had enough of burnt offerings . . . I do not delight in the blood of bulls, or of lambs, or of he-goats" (Isaiah 1, 11). "I hate, I despise your feasts, and take no delight in your solemn assemblies . . . Take away from me the noise of your songs; to the melody of your harps I will not listen. But let justice roll down like waters, and right-eousness like an everflowing stream" (Amos 5, 21–24).

What if one were to stand up and say, "Your Masses drive me to despair, your communions are excommunications, your sacraments are magic, stamps. It disgusts me." The prophets spoke in this way.

Jesus, through his Incarnation, as well as by his new commandment, indivisibly united the love of man with the love of God. Jesus desacralized everything except man. The Gospel is violent. It stirred things up in its time. *We* have covered it up with a layer of sacredness, so that it remain quiet, underneath. But Christ was a revolutionary against the sacred. He desacralized the Sabbath, the great Sabbath, Sunday! Can one work two hours, an hour and a half, three hours, and what kind of work? Servile, intellectual? Christ said, "The Sabbath is made for man and not man for the Sabbath." This saying is terrible. He desacralized the Temple, and for them it was really something! The Temple? Destroy it, in three days I will make you another, better one! This is blasphemy for a Jew. The Fast! People said: "Why don't your disciples fast?" He answered, "When the bridegroom is there it is not the moment to fast. Do not put my new wine in your old wineskins."

The first Christians scandalized pagans because they had no priests: they all were priests. They had no sacred places, no temple, they would have Mass anywhere . . .

Christ desacralized even worship:

"Go *first* and make peace with your brother. Leave the

altar. Leave the Mass. Leave God, and go make peace with your brother." And he said too, "What I want is mercy, not your sacrifices."

He wanted mercy, compassion, forgiveness, pity, the love of others—all of this before giving worship, before making sacrifice. A single thing defiles, from now on, and it is the refusal to love. For from now on, a single thing is sacred: man.

Our respect for man, our need of recuperating all men in the final beatitude, our certainty that if we love and save only one man (or lose him), we are doing something eternal —all of this is founded, not upon conjecture, but upon the historical and demonstrable fact of the Resurrection of Jesus Christ.

Jesus is the man in whom history reached its term in advance and who offers to associate us with the glorification of his humanity.

This historical fact has among us a consequence, a visible prolongation: sanctity. The saints show us a type of man who already shares the Resurrection of Christ.

More simply, each of us who has lived his faith has experienced a death and a resurrection. If you have made a true confession, celebrated a true Mass, prayed sincerely, if you have lived in a true Christian milieu, a group of adults who prayed and worked together, you have had this experience. You can be renewed, you can completely transcend yourself, you can be washed and regenerated, you can experience something so good, so true, so great that you know it for always. You feel that you are thus incorporating yourself, by effacing yourself, into the truth, the density, the eternity of this value which you affirm in dying.

We believe that truth is Someone, that love is Someone, and that all those who love and believe in him share his life and his eternity.

IV

The Service of Love

I

What I have said thus far has certainly raised some questions in your mind. I will now attempt to answer some of them.

A word first to those who may not have rightly understood my praise of fatherhood and my somewhat free translation of the Preface of the Holy Trinity.

Celibacy and virginity are first and above all a poverty, the poverty of one who does not even have a child, a husband, a wife of his own. In this poverty, clearly recognized, fully accepted, God can do great things. The true births are from God; the great fecundities are spiritual. In the Old Testament, when there was need of a remarkable child, he was almost always born of a sterile woman—and in the New Testament of a virgin. A purely physical fatherhood is the saddest, most criminal thing in the world! And there are, unfortunately, so many orphans in the world, spiritual orphans at least, whom no one has yet awakened to confidence, affection, joy, faith. There is indeed no lack of opportunity for the single person to exercise his or her paternal or maternal capacity.

However, the true problem of single people seems to me to be the following: under what conditions can a single person become an adult?

The true danger of celibacy is not sexual frustration (there are continent people who are happy and well-balanced), nor even affective isolation. The true danger is to remain infantile, capricious, selfish, discontented. An old bachelor, an old maid, is above all an old child. They have not matured because they have not committed themselves.

What is an adult?

Rather than giving a definition, I am going to propose a test to you. Which do you prefer: to love someone who does not love you, or to be loved by someone you do not love?

As soon as one has begun to understand the test, one becomes a little bit annoyed and protests: "I don't get it. *I* want to love someone who loves *me*."

But this is too good, it never happens. In the most united couple, the two never play the same tune. There is always one of them, at certain times in any case, who feels he loves more or loves alone. And sometimes they both feel that way at the same time. As a matter of fact, it is said that the greatest sacrifice for a wife is to accept that her husband love her in a way completely different from the way she loves him.

The true choice is the one I propose to you. In which case will you be happier: when you are loved, fêted, cherished, surrounded with love—or when you are capable of loving and attaching yourself to someone else.

Duhamel, in one of his novels, shows the family gathered around Cecile, the artist, the inspired member of the family, who plays the piano. As soon as she starts playing, each one automatically returns to his favorite dreams, isolates himself in his thoughts, is occupied again by his personal problems. The father thinks of women, the mother of her children and her domestic worries, another of the child she is expecting. But Justin thinks of Cecile, of his love for her, so painful, so hopeless. He thinks that she does not love him, that she will never love him, a Jew, a foreigner, obscure and ugly. He frets and worries.

But Cecile is a great artist. And under the sway of the music, all these dreams evolve, leave earth, arise; something inspired and luminous transforms them, and Justin thinks: How much I love Cecile, what a joy, what a blessing to know and to love her. *I* am the luckier of the two, she is poor: she does not love, she does not know this happiness. I will never be happy enough, thankful enough, kind enough to her. I love her. I have something to give her and, perhaps, to teach her. I would like her to be as happy as I am.

In an instant, under the influence of art, he has passed from childhood to adulthood.

For childhood is the selfish and acquisitive period par excellence. The baby treats himself as the center of the world.

He demands, sucks, swallows up, rejects, and bursts into rage and anxiety if something is refused to him. The universe is at his service. He only knows how to receive, to demand, to be loved, to take.

The adult is he who knows how to love, who knows how to give, to devote himself and to be happy enough to ask nothing in return.

Modern psychology expresses a profoundly Christian view when it says that the whole evolution of man is from infantile selfishness to adult generosity, from the need to be loved to the capacity for loving.

What was your answer to my test? What, above all, is your attitude in life?

The adult is he who has the initiative of love, who does not wait to be loved in order to love, who loves someone who does not love him, so patiently and faithfully that he will succeed in awakening the other to this love.

This is being a father, a mother: awakening, engendering persons to love.

"If you love those who love you, if you salute only your brethren, you do the same as tax collectors and Gentiles. But you, be like your heavenly Father . . ."

And this is what the single person is liable to lack: a commitment absorbing enough, a devotion demanding enough in order not to remain a "dabbler," capricious, compassionate for his own misfortunes and bad luck. A single person must find a (human) job, an occupation demanding enough for the mind and the heart, something, I dare to say, as

annoying as a husband, as demanding as a wife and children, which forms his character, makes him suffer in depth,
—in short, which draws from him all the love he is capable of.

Then he will become a genuine man or a genuine woman.

Marriage matures a person because it is unconditional
commitment ("unconditional surrender"), irreversible, in-
dissoluble. So the entire being employs and deploys itself in
order to meet it.

There is no other assurance of maturity and happiness.

The only assurance that God made towards us in creating
us is a kind of marriage (the new and eternal covenant):
I will love them so well, I will suffer from them so patiently,
I will forgive them so often that they will finally come to
know that I love them.

II

"You condemn individualism," you may object, "but isn't
the present danger precisely in its opposite—in the fact that
men are losing their individualism and becoming part of the
collective mass?"

Yes, but these two dangers are simultaneous; they rein-
force one another. History shows that individualism in society gives rise to fascism and tyranny, while collectivism
suppresses individual freedom and initiative. Both subordi-

nate the rights of the individual to those of the state. Only in a union of free and responsible persons can there be a society in which everyone can grow and develop.

I distinguish three stages of social life. Formerly the individual was surrounded by and committed to an active social life. He lived in towns or small cities. Everyone knew one another and, often, helped one another. There were true human relationships.

Nowadays the individual is a member of "mass society." Nowhere is solitude greater than in the multitude. Man is caught up in structures so vast and powerful, so completely anonymous, that he feels powerless, overwhelmed.

The usual reaction, characteristic of our time, is to dissociate oneself from all that is collective and take refuge in one's apartment or little house, to withdraw into one's family where you are still someone, where you count for something, and to worry about your little family happiness.

We have to create a new, personal civilization: to re-establish, to reinvent personal relations between men; not to let ourselves be blindly guided and crushed by anonymous administrative structures. To react, to associate in order to protest, control, humanize their functioning. Not to give in, but to unite in order to take the responsibility for all that others endure. To judge, to inform ourselves, to think, to organize movements and committees, to react against the feeling of helplessness which paralyzes our contemporaries and demonstrate everywhere that a few determined men and women can intimidate and sometimes transform social machineries which seem inexorable and all-powerful.

This is what you Christians should do wherever you are: structure anew a human society out of this multitude of irresponsible and powerless individuals.

Genuine modern asceticism, by the way, is neither fasting nor abstinence (it is, on the contrary, to sleep enough, to eat calmly, and to have distractions which are not more tiring than work!), but taking part in innumerable committees (providing that one is active in them!) and attending four or five different meetings a week. For the need for information, reflection, and social action is so great in our time that it is impossible to meet it without helping one another, without an active and continued collaboration.

"We are already so socialized," some people say when they are talking about the liturgy. "Our churches are the last refuge for solitude and silence, and you want to transform them into community meetings."

I answer: A true communal liturgy educates and arouses to personal prayer. I need the others in order to be myself. In every sphere, I am never more myself than when I am made to enter into myself by another: an artist, a philosopher, a writer, a saint.

Take reading, for example: the best moments of the book are those when I stop reading, when, going my way on the impulse which the book has given me, I invent my own thought, thanks to the genius of the author.

Of course, if I read a book without stopping, at great speed, in order to know the end, as for a detective story, I am not myself for a while, the reading has "alienated" me. But if you never read, you will be free to be fully yourself in the swamp of your solitary ruminations!

So, too, in liturgy, if an obnoxious commentator gabs to you from the beginning to the end of Mass, he excites people more to murder than to prayer. But if you have participated in a well-celebrated Mass, rendered transparent by the truth restored to each gesture, to each word, you will have been raised to a level of prayer which you would never have reached alone.

III

"How can you say that God is poor?"

What is it to be poor? To share, to welcome, to unite in solidarity with others. Has not God done all this? Has he not united in solidarity with us? Has he not welcomed us into the intimacy of his Trinity? The Father is he who gives everything, to the point of being pleased only in another. When he manifests himself in the theophanies of the New Testament, he speaks only of another, he directs us, not towards himself, but towards another: "This is my beloved Son, listen to him!"

The Son is he who has received everything, who has nothing of his own, who does not know how to do anything on his own, but only what he sees the Father do. Whoever sees him, sees the Father. The poverty of Christ on the straw of Bethlehem or on the cross of Calvary is a revelation, an expression of the profound and eternal reality of his being: he is rich only with the love of the Father. He, too, like our poor, lives on charity!

And the Holy Spirit does not speak on his own: he receives what is Christ's and announces it to us. He bears witness to another.

Humility, too, is a theological virtue. God is humble, but not only in that banal and logical sense that humility is truth, and that God knows himself as he is. In a deeper sense, humility is a consequence of love: it is to cease to attach importance to oneself, because one so loves and admires another. It is to be not self-satisfied; it is not to worry about one's glory.

Humility is not to strike a balance, even an exact balance, of one's shortcomings and qualities. It is to put one's delight so much in another that one no longer thinks of oneself.

I have been told that the first disillusion of a lover is sometimes to learn that the person he admired also took interest in him, could care for someone like him.

Humility is necessary, not only in order for us to know man, but for us to know God. Humility and poverty have the savor of God, for they are other names for love.

IV

"You say that God is poor and yet we say at Mass that the Father is almighty!"

The very question reveals him who asks it. He imagines God smiling at us, trying to get round us; but in case this ruse does not work he holds in reserve, as though it were a stick behind his back, his omnipotence! No, the omnipotence of God is one of fatherhood, a fatherly omnipotence.

How many people worship an idol! They project into God their desire: "Ah! if I were all-powerful" "Well, what would you do? Do you dare to say it? And that is what you imagine of God?"

The almighty God put all his happiness in his love, all his power in loving beings and arousing them to life. God is such a fatherly power, God has such a power of creation, God loves us so much that he creates us and resuscitates us unceasingly. As old and hardened as you may be, he is capable of making you his child once more. It is the first affirmation of Christ to the old and prudent Nicodemus.

The true atheist does not say that God does not exist. He says that God will no longer change him, that he has tried too often, that it is too late, that he is too old (and one says this at fifteen as well as at sixty). *He* denies the almighty Father, the omnipotence of the divine fatherhood.

When you call God Father, it is not an honorary title, it is the acknowledgement of a function, a power: he is capable of engendering sons and daughters; he loves you enough to resuscitate you as his child.

Our subtle way of denying this possibility is to think: there are others. God is Father because there are others, different from me, good, obedient, faithful children. But this attitude supposes that God, in order to make his children, finds in others good dispositions, good raw materials. Then you do not believe in the fatherly omnipotence! You reduce him to recognizing acquired values, to transforming what pre-exists.

To be Father is to draw forth from nothing, to love the first, to love before one is worthy of it. If God is truly a fatherly omnipotence, what he needs is not "prefabricated" sons and daughters. That would be somewhat like adopting them as adults. It would be awful.

No, he needs them to be half-formed, immature, miserable. He needs them to be stupid, stubborn, half-dead, or worse: he needs them as we are. It is then that he can show himself as the almighty Father! God alone can love us and give himself as he does.

God alone is communicable. A finite being cannot give himself totally to another without losing himself or the other. God alone is not one of us: he is deeper within us than we ourselves. He is infinitely "Person" (we are indefinitely, but not infinitely, communicable persons).

God could have manifested himself as transcendent by his Power, his lightning, his thunder, or by his intelligence, or his independence. But he chose to do it by what constitutes him most intimately: his love, his way of loving, that is, finally, through his Incarnation.

He is God, he is love, because he offers us everything, because he shares everything, because he proposes to us to become God, that is, to love like him, to be perfect as he is perfect.

You are shocked by this condescendence; you think that this proposition should not be taken literally, that God could not forget his rank like this?

But think of it: that in which God surpasses us most can only be what constitutes him most intimately: his love.

You think you must carefully keep at a distance from God in order to preserve his splendid isolation? But in just this way you lose the opportunity of experiencing how he is the most transcendent to you. Try to love like him! Let yourself be carried by him as far as you can—and it is then that you will experience, as never before, his transcendence! Who is capable of loving like him?

No doubt he will communicate his love to you—but you will know then that it is he who loves in you, he who does great things in the poverty of his servants.

God is God because he is love. He is never more God than when he loves us to the point of giving himself to us. We know God only through Jesus Christ. Do not try to reach God in any way other than through the Incarnation.

Read the Gospel: the Transcendent is someone who washes our feet! And if this scandalizes you and you look for something else, apply to yourself his threat to St. Peter when he,

like you, rebels and advises Jesus better to maintain his rank
and preserve his dignity: "If I do not wash you, you have
no part in me" (John 13, 8).

God has put his power on the cross so that one might
henceforth see nothing in him but his love. When you are
told that God loves you, you are told something so often
repeated, so worn out that it no longer means anything to
you. Translate it in a living way: God has given you power
over him. This is to love someone: to give him power over
you. When someone loves you, you have power over him,
power to rejoice him, to make him happy, satisfied; but also
power to make him suffer. And one loves to make use of
one's powers.

The Gospel, the Passion, was the revelation of the power
God had given us over him. One could do everything to
him, all that one can do to someone who has surrendered
himself to you, who is handed over to you.

God is weak before us. When Jacob had wrestled with the
angel, God imposed on him a new and prophetic name:
"Israel," which means: "Strong against God." We are the
true Israel. We are strong against God.

In Normandy there is this cynical and cruel motto: "He
who loves the least is always the strongest." In a married
couple there is always one who loves less than the other; he
is stronger, he keeps a cool head, he has control of the situation, he commands! God, towards us, will always be the
weaker: he loves us! He has cancelled his power.

Tyrrel says: "Man in revolt against God is the bird which,

amid the storm, throws itself against the cliff. But God in his compassion became flesh, so that the violence of the shock would be endured by him, and not by us."

But all this power which we exercise over him, usually to reduce him to silence, to flout him and humiliate him, we are free to use to honor him and rejoice him. "I honor my Father," Jesus said. "You dishonor me."

The only efficacious motive for going to pray in church, the only perpetual reason for going to confession, is not that it pleases you (one would wait a long time!), but that it pleases him, that you are certain thus to touch his heart and rejoice him.

This is how God loves us and the extent to which he invites us to join him. Try it!

V

I have been asked how one can love "unbearable" people and whether to love someone for the love of God is to love God.

Do you know what Docetism is? It is a very widespread heresy, not limited to the early Church, which professes that the Word pretended to become incarnate. He only took on the appearance of man.

I find this heresy still alive today. There are Christians who believe that Christ took on a human body, but does not have a human soul. And there are even theologians and exegetes who believe that Christ is so much God that he cannot be truly man.

For them, as one of my friends jokingly puts it, Christ is someone who pretends to ride a mere bicycle to encourage the cyclists, but who has a motor-bike! So he feigns to push on the pedals, he sighs from time to time to look tired, he mops his face because the others sweat . . . but he has a motor-bike! He pretends to be man, but behind there is God *Omnipotens!*

"Jesus grew in wisdom, stature and grace." Bossuet comments: "Jesus possessed all perfection from birth, but he let it appear only progressively in order to resemble a genuine child."

And in how many authors have I read that Jesus prayed, not because he needed to but "to set us a good example"!

Well, there is also a docetism of the love of one's neighbor: "To love one's neighbor as if he were God." And God keeps fictitious records: he will reward you as if it were he whom you helped. Since God pretended to become incarnate in Jesus Christ, he can just as well pretend to have been helped in the least of his children.

But Christ did not say, "All that you have done to the least of these, it is as if you had done it to me." He said, "You did it to me!" Just as he said "This is my Body" and not "Pretend that it is my Body."

God became incarnate loyally.

But how can I love a man as I love God? Under the same condition under which you would have loved the God-man:

believing in him! In order to love someone with a theological love, it is necessary to believe in him, to believe in a presence of God in each man. Without faith, charity hesitates and mistrusts itself.

To love someone is to believe, to hope in him forever. You stop loving someone from the moment you claim to know him. If a wife believes that she knows her husband, and above all if a husband believes that he knows his wife, from the moment they no longer expect anything from one another, when they no longer give credit to everything new, better, unforeseeable that may emerge from a spiritual being who needs no less than eternity to show what he has in his heart, they have stopped loving each other.

VI

To judge someone is to kill him. In the Gospel, the phrase "Do not judge" means do not identify someone with what you know of him. Give him credit. One must judge in a sense, one must know people. One must not be blind. We must not think that in order to love people we must avoid seeing their shortcomings. For, in this case, you love your charity, you love loving them, but you do not love *them.* One must see them; charity is not a blindness, but a higher lucidity. One must see them in their entirety: as they are, but as I believe them too, as I know them through my faith. In other words, we must respect in each one the God who is present and who is waiting to be discerned in him in order to grow. To love someone, I must give him credit. I must believe that he is capable of changing.

Do you believe in the almighty Father, in a love in which you take part, which is capable of awakening the other, of changing him, of awakening him to life. Do you give credit to this love? Do you have faith, the faith which teaches us that God communicates himself to each person?

We are far from the usual arguments: "God commands us to love the others. It is a command, therefore I do it." How arbitrary!

When I say that God loves the others, that means: God communicates himself to the others. It means Incarnation, Redemption, Resurrection.

F. X. Durwell, the theologian of the mystical body, says: "Christ rose as a mystical body." He became flesh again in each of us. He is still individual, personal. He is still a person, but he is a person extensive to all other persons. He is all-powerful in love to the point of reaching all those he loves. He lives in each person. He proposes himself to each person. He enlightens every man who comes into this world. With all his strength he tempts him, with all the reality of his love.

Many people hesitate to believe in the presence of the Lord in the sinner, but it is above all there that he is. He has only been working in there, since the creation of the world—in the sinner. He attaches himself to the sinner with all his strength.

God never becomes discouraged. A father, a mother does

65

not become discouraged. Since the Incarnation Christ has united himself in solidarity with all men. The Greek Fathers consider that "through the Incarnation of Christ, there is something changed in human nature." In every man there is a real influence of Christ, a call which changes his destiny even if he refuses it. There is a fine point of his being where his Redemption is virtual, where the love of God invades him at least enough to solicit him.

Who can boast of totally refusing God? That amounts to total consent! No one escapes totally from God. No one is clearsighted enough, vigilant enough, to recognize him and refuse him under all the faces under which he presents himself to us. You may say "no" to him under the aspect of a priest, say "no" to him under the aspect of the Church, of morality, of Christian politics, it is possible not to love him under all these faces. But perhaps you love the poor, perhaps you cannot stand injustice, perhaps you are sensitive to the freshness of a child, to innocence, to purity, perhaps you appreciate nature, perhaps you experience affection, pity, admiration? Under all these forms you have said "yes" to God! You did not recognize him, but never mind. They were realities of God.

We say that we are open to God, and yet there is a great deal of resistance. One says neither a total yes nor a total no. In the same way these fellows are not in a state of grace but they are infiltrated with grace, threatened by grace, surrounded with grace, shot through with grace, shot through with the patient, humble, immense love of God.

"Behold, I stand at the door and knock," says the Apocalypse. "If anyone hears my voice and opens the door, I will come in to him and eat with him, and he with me" (3, 20). I will love him so well, I will suffer from him so patiently, I will forgive him so often, that he finally will come to know that I love him.

Claudel says magnificently: "None of our brothers, even if he should want to, is capable of failing us, and within the coldest miser, at the center of the prostitute and of the dirtiest drunkard, there is an immortal soul holily breathing which, though excluded from the day, practices nocturnal adoration."

There is in every person a zone, a garden of innocence and integrity, where God speaks and where one does not entirely know how to keep from responding.

Newman, attending the agony of some of his unbelieving friends, interprets their anguish by saying that they realized that they were going to lose, for the first time and forever, a grace of presence, affection, and love which had given to their life all its fecundity, all its inner warmth, to which they never wanted to open themselves. All their life, they had been bathed by this proposition of presence, by this discreet affection, by this humble solicitation, and they had enjoyed it without opening themselves.

The only way to love people is to love them at this depth. In every person God exists, God lives. He is waiting to be discerned in order to grow in him. But this depth resounds only at the call of our own innocence. This presence of God in others is awakened only by the living faith with which we call upon it.

VII

You should become so transparent to the presence of God in you that you bear witness that he is living and that you come to others naked, vulnerable, disarmed, with this presence which appeals to theirs. That is what saints do in the world. Wherever saints go, the world is threatened. The approach of the saints is threatening. The citadels of lust and hate with which sinners fortify themselves crumble before someone who loves them and is not afraid.

Those who look at the world with faith save the world. Charity is not a pious blindness, it is a higher passion and lucidity. To see one's neighbor as he is, is to see him inhabited by God, with all his shortcomings, tempted like you, tempted by God. It is to see God, as it were, cramped for room in him, and trying to come out in the open.

The whole Christian adventure is to attempt to give birth to God in the world. Have you given birth to your husband, your wife, your children? How many times will you have to give birth to them, to love them enough to give them birth anew? You will have to begin believing in them anew. Even when they seem the least deserving, they will be poor helpless things who are begging for deliverance, who beg you to comfort them for having been so undeserving. You know very well how to do this with children, why do you not know how to do it with others? Adults are children. They need to be loved in order to be good.

V

Church and Resurrection

I

We have centered religion on the God-man; we have laid great stress on the sacred character of man.

Nature has been desacralized: in contrast with the pagan religions which divinized nature, imposed respect for it, and advised submission to it, Christianity teaches that man must dominate the world. Science and technology have religious value for us because they fulfill a first commandment of God. God is creator, God is worker, and man is in the image of God because he completes the world. If God rested on the seventh day, after the creation of man, it is because he had finally found someone who would take care of what remained to be done!

Religious practices have been desacralized. Our religion is in spirit and in truth. The Sabbath is made for man, the sacraments are made for man, and not man for the sacraments. Sin is lack of love.

Only man is an irreplaceable and inviolable sacredness. Our love and our respect for God will be judged on our love and respect for man.

I have said this over and over again—but I hope you have not been putting on airs about it!

I recall the Gospel passage where someone comes to tell the Lord: "Your mother and your brothers are outside asking for you." Instead of getting up, Christ asks, "Who are my mother and my brothers? . . . Whoever does the will of God is my brother, and sister, and mother" (Mark 3, 32–35).

Then, I imagine, those present felt well at ease. But Mary, apparently neglected, kept this word and meditated on it in her heart.

Thus, at Calvary, she alone whom this word had hurt, she alone whom this word had penetrated like a sword, she alone was there.

And all the others, who had gloried in this word, had disappeared.

Well, in the same way, when I tell you that man is the best dwelling of God, and that the most beautiful manifestation of the glory of God is man living God's life—I hope that I hurt you, that everyone looks back over his life to reproach himself for living of it so little.

If God wants to become incarnate in you, what time, what

room, what welcome have you offered him up until now?

The great means by which God communicates himself is prayer. The time during which you pray is the time of God's Incarnation in you.

I dislike the word "contemplation." Christianity is not contemplation; it is infinitely more: it is participation. God is not an object for your gaze, or your search. He is the cause, the grace, the motor of it. He is not above all loved but loving! If you pray, it is because he calls you to it, it means that his grace is working in you and has already won this first and surprising victory: to have led you to pray!

In prayer, you participate, God associates you with the worship he renders himself, to the murmur of love, confidence, joy, gratitude, which rises from the heart of the Son towards the Father.

And in action, God associates you with the love with which he loves the world and men.

If you pray without acting, it means that you have not prayed to the true God "who acts unceasingly," "who so loves the world," "who sends his son into the world."

But if you act without praying, if you give *yourself* a mission, you will be able to carry to others only a pitiful message: yourself! It is not you who should go to others, it is God who must have become living enough in you so that you will bear witness to his love and not to yours. It is above all in action that one must be . . . contemplative!

God alone is communicable, you can give nothing of

yourself. But you can permit others to find God. One cannot give less than God and one can give nothing but God. Man is sacred, but he has to be penetrated by the sacred. So let yourself be penetrated, be silent a little. Die a little. Pray, be quiet before him. Sit down. Let yourself become sacred. It is certain that man is the only thing sacred. But he is so very little. He puts up a good resistance to the sacred. What of God have you let infiltrate into you? What does one see upon seeing you? Is it God? "He who sees me sees the Father!" Have you died and risen?

The proof of the Resurrection of Christ, the only proof for our contemporaries, is that you live a little of God, is that you emerge more alive from your confessions, from the chapel, from your baptism, from your prayer. When Christ came back from praying, the apostles would say: "What's with him, what happened? Where did he go?" He went to pray. If *we* only knew how to pray! If we could only pray in this way! "Lord, wouldn't you like to teach us to pray?"

Notice that Christ never had his disciples pray before they asked him for it. They had no prayer meetings, no processions, nothing. But he would often pray all night long, and finally they said, "We would like to become like him. We would like to learn to pray like him." What a good method of education for fathers. He never forced his children to pray but he prayed so well (not even in front of them) that, at his return, they would say, "What happened?

He is no longer the same." He no longer was the same. He was living of something else. He was radiant.

How is it to be like you? Do others want to become like you? Go get rid of your sad face! Go get another face!

One more word on poverty and asceticism. There is no recipe for poverty. You will always be poor at poverty. You will never find yourself poor enough. You will always have to ask yourself this question and to impoverish yourself till the end of your days. One becomes genuinely poor only without noticing it.

Beware of the dangerous spiritual illness which I call "perfectitis," the excessive worry about attaining perfection. It is the story of the fellow who absolutely wants to get on board the train of perfection, and who, seeing it pulling off and picking up speed when he is still on the platform, loaded down with all his baggage, makes an heroic decision, drops his suitcases, and leaps onto the train.

But as the train moves along, the joy at having caught it diminishes, and the thought of the suitcases becomes distressing. The memory of one object after another upsets him and draws him back. At a certain degree of obsession, there is only one thing left for him to do: jump out and go get his suitcases.

One must not tear these possessions away from oneself; they must become progressively useless. God takes it unto himself to divest you of them in his gentle, affectionate, patient way, if you are willing to follow him or listen to him. "Another will gird you and carry you where you did not wish to go" (John 21, 18). A gentle hand will take your hand, other hands will stretch out to you, and take hold of yours. You will love them so well, you will meet such good people around you, that you will not be able not to share. Do not begin by being poor. Begin by loving them. Begin by being happy. Have a reasonable comfort, sensible recreation. But above all have friends who value other things besides comfort and recreation.

An enormous amount of common sense is needed to do good. What is unfortunate is that, generally, as soon as people become good they automatically become so stupid! It would seem that the effort they make to practice virtue tires them or exempts them from using their intelligence. As soon as they think they are inspired by the Holy Spirit, they lose the little they had when they were low and mean-spirited.

Even our Lord complains about it. "The sons of this world are wiser in their own generation than the sons of light" (Luke 16, 8). Yet he had warned us, in order to do good, to be "as prudent as serpents, and as simple as doves." Which some Christians realize by becoming as ugly as dragons, and as silly as geese!

Four gifts of the Holy Spirit concern intelligence, four out of seven! Intelligence, wisdom, counsel, and knowledge. Does this not imply that in order to serve and devote oneself, one needs prudence, sagacity, experience, common sense, human and Christian wisdom?

This reminds me of a professor who in class was making a speech on sacerdotal vocation, and in order to make us measure its greatness he added this argument: "And the priest studies for a long time. Very few liberal professions demand so many years of intellectual formation . . ." "Sir," a wise guy interrupted, "maybe they need it more than others!"

If the Holy Spirit has destined four gifts for the common sense of Christians . . . it is perhaps because they need them more than others!

II

We are all subjects of Incarnation. But I am going to speak about the Incarnation of God where he is most incarnate: in the Church. He is incarnate in every man in a certain but peripheral way, since many men refuse him, struggle against him. But where he is especially incarnate, what he especially made sacred, consecrated, sacralized (it is the same thing), is the Church. He promised her his perpetual, indefectible presence. I have spoken of Incarnation only because of the Church. The Church is the very center of Incarnation. I am a man of the Church because I am for the religion of Incarnation.

If I left the Church, I would break with Christ and at once become an *idealist*. I would have tremendous projects, magnificent ideas, and I would pass just beside reality. Like the man who wants to convert everybody but neglects his wife. Like the woman who wants to convert everyone but neglects her husband. Like the man who arrives in a parish and wants to transform it but cannot stand his pastor. Idealists!

The weight of the Church upon me is precisely the weight of the reality of the Incarnation: my God is not a God whom I invent.

If the Church were to my taste, it would not be the true Church. I would have invented it. If it were satisfying, it would only be human. There must be an element in it which is beyond me. In your life, do you not feel that God never wants what you want! He is always different from what you thought. When you are faithful to your vocation, to your plan of life, it annoys you, it hurts you. Because God is demanding. The Church is demanding, it makes one suffer. If you only love someone perfect, you love no one. If you only obey those who are right, you never obey. And if you believe in something obvious, you do not believe. The Church is the source of all my religious life. I have received everything from it, I have learned everything from it. Little by little. And what gives me such confidence is that it took me a great deal of time to understand a great many things, and each time I experienced, thanks to the Church, a human and religious deepening. All that I have understood has been in the Church, because of it, bringing me closer to it. It is the milieu of my faith. It is there that I have found everything, received everything, and there that I know I still have everything to learn. In the Church's sacraments, in its words, in its communities of love, in him whom, in spite of all, it represents.

One must know how to suffer from the Church, as one suffers from those one loves, as in a marriage. For him who loves, a thousand objections do not make one doubt, and for him who does not love, a thousand proofs do not make a certainty.

Your fidelity will always make you suffer. Have you noticed in the Gospel that Christ yearned for the pagans? He was bound to his community of Israel. He could not go out of it, but he yearned for the pagans and said, "Woe to you, Chorazin! Woe to you, Bethsaida! For if the mighty works done in you had been done in Tyre and Sidon, they would have repented long ago in sackcloth and ashes" (Matthew 11, 21). And when he met someone really good, he would say: "This is marvellous, I have never seen this kind of thing in Israel before. I have never seen this in my community. I have never seen this among Catholics."

And yet Christ remained bound to his community. He remained faithful to it unto the cross, unto death, and he saved it, *his* Church. But he sometimes had yearnings. He found that it was rugged going in his Church, that the people were hard. But he loved them and he saved them. If he had gone away, he would no longer have loved. If you want to love as you please, you will love no longer.

To believe in the Church is to believe that God lives in

it, acts in it, acts in it more than anywhere else. To believe is at once to have experienced it and to expect it again— but both together. How can you give an experienced, existential content to acts of faith, hope, and charity by simply reciting the definitions which the Church gives for them? We need a certain experience of what this way of loving is . . . and it is the Holy Spirit who makes us love in this way.

In the same way, if in prayer or in a true confession, you have not experienced what a Resurrection is, what I have said will have no meaning for you. Are you sometimes resurrected? Are you sometimes washed, renewed?

Well, it is above all in the Church that the resurrecting energy of Christ exercises itself on you and on the Church itself. I believe that the Church at every moment, in every century, must die and be raised again. It must abandon its aged forms, its compromises, its sins. It must immerse itself again in the purifying river and rise again new, pure, without spot or wrinkle, but holy and without blemish before God. And we are now witnessing such a Resurrection. The Church in renewal is the Resurrection of Christ. He dies in it and rises in it. And in the Church of today, there are great promises of Resurrection. It is germinating and blooming everywhere. How many coincidences, how many providential correspondences! Everywhere in the Churches the same complaints, the same propositions, wishes, desires are rising. It is the work of the same Spirit.

Biblical, liturgical, theological renewal, conjugal renewal, community renewal, the spirituality of laymen and of earthly realities, are just so many outbursts, so many striking effusions of the Holy Spirit. Do you have faith in the Church? Do you believe that she is capable of rejuvenating? Do you have faith in your wife, your husband, your neighbors, your community, in those you care for? It is your faith in the Church, it is your faith in those who are closest to you: your children, your parents, your neighbors, your parish, which will make them rise from the dead, which will make of them all a true Church. We have faith in the God who can raise the dead, who makes us go through his mystery of death and resurrection. We should not wonder that the Church goes through periods of eclipse. But she has in her the force of resurrection of Christ; she has always been resurrected.

III

The characteristic of the Christian religion is that God reveals himself to men, at man's level, at man's height. The astonishing thing about Christianity is that God is known to us under a sensible form. For a moment this fact should shock you, for God is said to be obscurity, darkness, God demands obedience and faith. And yet it is much more true to say that God is light, revelation, manifestation, epiphany. The Christian religion differs from every other by the fact that it is a religion of incarnation, a sacramental religion.

The Church is neither materialistic nor idealistic, she is sacramentalistic. This means: she believes that God invades us through sensible means. The creation of man in the image and resemblance of God already prepared this communication.

The Fathers of the Church said, "When God formed the body of Adam, he was already thinking of Christ who would one day be man." He made man permeable to God.

Have you noticed that, in the Bible, God always made himself incarnate? Even in Paradise God manifested himself under a sensible form: he would talk familiarly with Adam, in the evening breeze. God would confide in Adam. Adam entered into God's confidence. God already surrendered himself in Paradise. He surrendered himself and was betrayed. The Passion, that is, the revelation of the bold, vulnerable love of God, began in Paradise.

Adam rejected the Revelation, he cut off the communication, and he became darkness. Sin is the state in which God is no longer known, no longer felt—you know that state well! It is an abnormal state. Normally, God is sensible, to the senses and to the heart! It is the darkness which does not grasp God, which refuses to grasp him. But "happy are the pure in heart! They see God!" They feel at ease near him. Still today, "his sheep hear his voice and follow him."

But God did not let himself be discouraged. Adam had taken refuge behind his curtain of leaves. God went to look for him: "Come on, what are you doing there? Come back, don't stay like that. It is so sad when you leave me. Come back, you know that I don't hold it against you. It's not worthwhile to stay in your corner. I will call you so well that you will nonetheless end up by hearing me and wanting to come back. So come back now!" God is like that.

Adam came back at once. Redemption is immediate. It is as "original" as sin! It is God who confessed Adam. And, as with us, he did much more than forgive him, he led him to have the desire and the courage to ask for forgiveness!

God continued to confide, to speak through the prophets. Moses spoke to God face to face, as a man speaks with his friend. The Israelites would never have crossed the desert if they had not had God with them. At that time, too, there were "sacraments": an ark in which God dwelled, a column of fire which preceded them at night, a column of clouds by day: God was leading them. They would never have gotten over all the obstacles, forty years of trial, if they had not had their God with them, the tabernacle, the manna, the real Presence! You will never go through the desert of your life without a sensible presence of God among you!

The veil which man had lowered was raised little by little by God until the Incarnation. *This* is the "revelation": God became fully visible. And the Incarnation is everlasting. "I am with you everyday." Guardini says so well, "Epiphany, Incarnation, sacraments are constant exigencies of the Christian life." God has decided to reach us as we are, in our mankind. It is for this reason that he made a Church. St. John marvels, "That which we have heard, which we have seen with our eyes, which we have looked upon and touched

81

with our hands, concerning the word of God" (1 John 1, 1). This is what Christ announces to us. This is the true religion. One touches, drinks, eats, nestles against God.

Happy are the pure in heart, they see God. The normal state, the natural human condition is to see God, to perceive him in what is sensible, what is usual, what is familiar. God is with us forever. The liturgy is an epiphany of God for each of us who attends it with an open heart: "The Word dwells among us, and we have beheld his glory."

In a true Mass, one sees his glory. You say so after the Gospel: "Praise to you, O Christ." Be sincere—have you seen his glory? Did the Gospel last Sunday say anything to you?

What is the Gospel? God who comes to live among men. He is still living among men. He is still the same. Men are still the same. The Gospel reveals to me how God speaks to me, how God treats me, how God lives at my side, and how *I* ignore him and maltreat him. The Gospel is closed and useless for you as long as you have not recognized yourself in it, as long as it has not unmasked you, as long as it has not said to you, "This man is you, *you* are doing this, *you* are resisting, abandoning, betraying . . ." *We* are the inhabitants of Bethlehem who have no room for Christ. If it is I who have done all this, I understand very well what happened. Today too I have no room for him, and in my day I do not have one hour to pray, I have no room, I have no time. And I know now why he is so poor, in his manger. It is I who have not given him anything, who have kept all my good clothes for myself. And I know why he is lying on the straw, and I know why he is on a cross. Let him be removed, let him be carried away; we will pretend not to know anything about it. One has no use for him. He hampers us by asking for our time.

"It is no longer because of your words that we believe, for we have heard for ourselves, and we know that this is indeed the Saviour of the world" (John 4, 42).

When I was young I would say to myself, "He saved the world two thousand years ago and we apply his merits," now I say that there is in the world, today, a force of salvation. He is saving the world today. There is a force of salvation which is going about in the world, I have seen it operating much more in others than in me, but I have seen it and I have seen people who knew it.

This word has sometimes spoken to me and it cannot be forgotten: it is living. As long as you have not heard it speaking, it is useless to say at Mass, "Glory to you, O Lord."

Did you behold his glory last Sunday? It was the same thing when Christ was there, when he was speaking. Some were there, their hearts closed, as spectators, very often as critics, carrying on a kind of mental debate with the speaker, in order to find his weak point, to find the answer, to fill up the hole he was digging, quick, quick. And when he had finished, they had not retained anything, except perhaps an objection.

But others were there, their hearts open, they let his word enter and it hurt and it did them good. They had never been as hurt, and they had never been as happy as when he was speaking, and they would have liked to stay there forever. And when he had finished, they would be asked, "What did he say? Why are you so overwhelmed, so transformed?" "I don't know, no man ever spoke like this man." They had beheld his glory; but for that one needs a pure heart.

"Happy are the pure in heart, for they shall see God."

IV

What else does the Church give us in order to see God more closely? She celebrates the sacraments.

"Since the Lord is no longer visible among us, all of him that was visible has passed into the sacraments," says St. Leo the Great.

What does Christ do in his sacraments? He consecrates men; he fills them with his life, his presence, his action.

To be sure, the Holy Spirit infiltrates men who do not pray, who do not make use of the sacraments, who do not read the word of God . . . but if you want to be completely consecrated, if you want a complement of consecration, then listen to his word, let yourself be penetrated by his word, communicate with his word. And this word is active.

Have you ever thought, regarding the reading of the Gospel, that the true Gospel of Mass is not the Gospel read to you in the first part of Mass? This one prepares the other, the true Gospel which is the consecration.

The consecration is a passage of the Gospel, read, proclaimed, listened to with so much faith that it realizes what it means. The word becomes active once more. It is listened to and received in faith. It becomes efficacious, it acts, it transubstantiates.

Do you listen to the word of God? Do you let it act? All the sacraments are but words of God become, once more, efficacious.

You say before communion (but you do not believe it), "Say but a word and my soul will be healed!"

Have you ever experienced this affirmation? If not, go tell lies wherever you want.

You go to propose your faith to others, but where does it come from? Have you heard him for yourself? Do you believe in God or in those who have spoken of him to you? How do you know that he is the Saviour of the world? Has he saved you? Are you a witness of the Resurrection? Shame on the religion which has but witnesses of the past! We need witnesses of the present. We need people who will say, "Christ is risen, he has resurrected me. He is the Saviour of the world." "How do you know?" "He has saved me! I have seen him save people!" But not people who will say, "He saved the world two thousand years ago. I am going to give you the proof of it. Let's go over to the public library!"

He saves in the sacraments. He becomes living again. He

acts in the sacraments. In confession! How does God mani-
fest himself in confession? How can he become living? You
hate to go to confession? No one wants to go! Why? Because there are two religions, the pagan and the Christian.

The first, the false one, is the religion of what one does
for God: efforts, sacrifices, mortifications which man does
for God. And one does so much that, in the end, one has
towards him a mentality of a rancorous benefactor. I have
done a great deal for him . . . But I wonder what he has
done for me. Many Christians have the mentality of rancorous benefactors towards God. Their religion consists in
the poor, sad, weak things they have done for God.

The other religion is the religion of the great things God
does for us. The great things he does in the poverty of his
servants. They are the *mirabilia Dei,* the sacraments, the
miracles. The miracles are renewed in the sacraments. It is
in them that you are resurrected. They resurrect the dead
every day. There are many more miracles in a confessional
than in all the pools of Lourdes. But people go more will-
ingly to Lourdes than they go to the confessional.

The true religion consists in the great, the wonderful
things that God does for us. And we will never know them
enough. We will never witness them enough.

Then why is your confession so annoying? Because your
confession is you! It is what *you* do, it is what you think:
"I am going to scour my conscience! . . . and it is no fun!
. . . And I am going to tell someone whom I know too
little or too well some disagreeable things . . . and then I

am going to do my penance . . ." Zero for you! Judas confessed in this way; he said: "I have sinned in betraying innocent blood." And he went and hanged himself.

What is confession? It is God about to tell you how he loves you. It is God about to make of you again his son or his daughter. It is God rejoicing at seeing you! *You* do not rejoice at seeing him. It is God rejoicing at being able to resurrect his child, to take him again in his arms, and to make him living! to give him life again. It is God waiting for you, hoping for you! It is God loving you! *God* makes you come to confession! and he has to pull! . . . because he likes to forgive you! He likes confession! (He is certainly the only one!) To go to confession is to witness this manifestation of the love of God which is capable of resurrecting ours.

A student once said to me, "Father, either confession is of no use, and then one should not confess; or it is of some use . . . but then I should not always have the same sins to tell."

I answered, "*You* want to confess in order not to have to confess again. You want to use God in order to do without him. You want to use God in order not to sin any longer. In order to edify your moral stature, after which you will be able to put God on leave . . . saying: Thank you, God, you have helped me a lot. You can go now." God does not string along with this bargaining, this farce. God wants to do no less in the sacrament of penance than reveal himself to you. The depth of the heart of God is revealed in forgiveness, because forgiveness is the supreme gift, it is the perfection of giving. If we were not sinners, needing forgiveness even more than bread, we would not know the depth of the heart of God, just as a child does not know the depth of his mother's heart if he is not invalid, if he has not been sick. He who is not forgiven does not love. It is Christ who said it: "He who is forgiven a little begins to love a little" (this is your stage, I suppose, of confession, of frequentation of confession, and your temperature of charity), "but he who is forgiven much, is shown so much love that he finally awakens to all the love he has been shown. He loves much."

Which do you prefer? Not to sin and not to know the depth of the heart of God? Or to sin and to know the extent to which he loves you? Do you want to be happy with yourself or happy with God? For me the worst sin is to avoid sinning in order not to have to go to confession. I mean the wise calculation in order to protect oneself, to do without God, in order not to give God the opportunity of showing himself a father. Confession manifests the extent to which God loves you. Well, you still have to sin a lot in order to know this love, and to go to confession a lot.

"But I always fall into the same sins!" It is perhaps that you have not yet understood the kindness with which God forgives you for them. You will have to sin a great deal yet before you know it and this is painful because you wanted to be happy with yourself and you will have to learn to be happy with God.

You will go to heaven, not because you are happy with yourself but because you are happy with God. You will go to heaven only if your faults become happy faults. You will go to heaven only if you have seen the glory of God in forgiveness. In heaven there are only forgiven sinners, happy about their forgiveness, enthusiastic about their confessor!

Others object, "Confession is tedious because I always have the same things to say."

Would you like to invent new faults, unprecedented sins, to leave your confessor breathless with astonishment?

No, the same things can be said over and over again without weariness—providing that they are true. Think of lovers, for example. Their conversations are quite monotonous. But for them they are fascinating!

The true motive of your boredom is that you say nothing in your confession—nothing true, nothing which you really care about.

Often I stop people in confession to suggest, "Be silent for only a moment. If you were to encounter Christ, if you could ask him for a miracle, a transformation, what would you ask of him?" Then people realize that they would have said nothing to Christ about what they say at confession. What they say is to please the priest, because one has to say something, but they feel that they would not have said that to Christ because it is not serious. They would not have dared to say such nonsense.

And then sometimes they say something true: that they have never accepted their financial situation, their life, their husband, their children, their parents, a death, a catastrophe, a failure, their face, their health, their character. That they have never believed in God. That they had never believed he was living, and above all that they had not believed he loved them in this way.

If they had seen Christ, they would have understood at once that they did not believe in him. And above all that they did not know he loved them, that it was he who was looking for them. *He* called on Zacchaeus in order to confess him: "Ho! Zacchaeus, my friend! What are you doing up there?" And the other said, "What's going on? He knows me? He calls me by my name and treats me like an old friend!"

Zacchaeus was dazzled with joy: he was loved. So he gave everything, he no longer needed anything. Do you know why you sin? Because you are empty, so you have to fill up your emptiness, with anything!—even with sins you are not so proud of. But what would you have had in your life, if you had not had your sins! After all, you had to fill this emptiness. And if you are empty, you will recommence your sins. But if God loves you, if he is your friend . . . and if you remain with him forever, *he* can fill your life. You feel at ease with him, you are happy. If his kindness has manifested itself, if you have seen his glory, you feel much better that way, you no longer need to sin, it is no longer necessary.

Zacchaeus gave everything and he wondered how he could have had the least interest in saving up all this money. He had found something better. What ought to happen in the confessional is that we discover something better than our sins. We would then be set free: *this* is the forgiveness of sins.

We would be dispensed from sinning because we would have found something so much better: the Father, the love of the Father. With this love, one can live, it is nourishing. But as long as you have not found it you have simply gone through the rite of confession, you have made the gestures. But you have not known the Father. So you have not known forgiveness.

VI

The Grace of Life

I

In the early Church, only public sinners were subjected to the forty days of Lenten penance. But at their solemn reconciliation, on Holy Thursday, they appeared so happy, renewed, luminous, they were so radiant with joy, with new innocence and fervor, that the other faithful would envy them and regret not having been sinners and penitents like them. Little by little all asked to bear the cross of ashes of Lent, all wished to become public penitents, so beautiful and beneficial it was to be reconciled in this way. But the sacrament of penance took forty days!

Now you obtain it in two minutes, but it really gives no one the desire to imitate you!

It is the only sacrament without liturgy. Not even a passage of the Gospel is read to you.

The average man is unable, by himself, to examine his conscience suitably; he ignores his main faults which are, generally, faults of omission. But if the sacraments were again to become communal, things would be quite different; we would enlighten one another! From time to time married people come to confess together. I can assure you that the examinations of conscience are well done. A collective preparation is indispensable in order to make a true judgment of one's own life.

Secondly, the average believer is unable to repent by himself. Passages of the Gospel ought to be read to him; the word of God ought to be proclaimed to him; what he has lost should be revealed to him, and he should be given the desire to come back.

And finally, he is unable to make reparation all by himself. All this ought to become communal again, except the avowal, though it is not as sensational as you imagine. The avowal of sins is secondary, though in our times it has been made the essential part. The very name of the sacrament shows this distortion: "Confession." But the true name of the sacrament is the Forgiveness of Sins.

We have forgotten that the sacrament is above all an act of God, a gesture of love and compassion by God. We have emphasized the (painful) gestures of man instead. Confession is what you do: "*I* confess."

There ought to be such a celebration of the forgiveness of sins that it would make the love of God *sensible*. It would wake us up, resurrect us to the love which God has for us.

II

There are three guarantees in the Church: that of the sacraments—it is nearly total: their efficacy fortunately does not depend on the worth of the priest who administers them.

The magisterium is already less guaranteed: the area in which it is infallible is strictly limited. There are only a few dogmas and the rest of the teaching is a function of the worth of the men who transmit it.

As for jurisdiction (the power of commanding), there is an ultimate guard-rail: in spite of all the errors of its leaders, the Church will never perish!

Do not confuse jurisdiction and the infallibility of the magisterium: "The pope decrees it, we have to believe in it." No, one must not believe in it, one must obey. And precisely, one truly obeys only if one does not believe in it. If you have to believe that the order is just, you never obey!

You must understand and appreciate the order which is given to you; you even have the right and sometimes the duty to make your difficulties respectfully known. But you must obey.

To separate yourself from the Church would be to separate yourself from Christ, to rend the communion of charity which he wants among all his members. And what will you represent then? Will you preach in your own name? Will you preach a doctrine of love and union which you have already denied?

The Church is the organism of salvation, the continuity of the message, the living presence of Christ, manifested through the gathering of its members. Christ wanted a visible Church; he therefore wanted a visible unity and we must profess it. To this end he has subjected us to fallible men. We cannot dissimulate either our duty of obedience or their fallibility.

III

What is lacking in our time is a lay spirituality: a spirituality of professional work, and a spirituality of conjugal life. Almost all Christians have the spirituality of the religious. They feel ill at ease, religiously speaking, in their life of work and in their conjugal life.

When you say to an average Christian, "Tell me where you stand in your religious life," you can be pretty sure he is going to answer by providing a list of his religious practices. Whereas the principal commandment of God is to love!

Your religious life is to love your wife, your husband, your work. How do you love your wife, your husband, your children, your work? You are no closer to God than you are to your work. You do not respect God any more than you respect your professional and conjugal life. You are the same distance from God that you are from your work, your wife, your children. You do not love God any better than you love your work. You do not love God any better than you love his will, his mission, what he has entrusted to you. You will therefore be judged above all on the way you have accomplished it. "He who does the will of my Father . . ." The will of the Father for you is your work. Your religious life is your work and it is in it that you are religious. What is it to be religious? You are the missionary of the Father, you are sent by the Father. You are charged with a mission by the Father. You accomplish the will of the Father!

No one ever confesses that he does not like his work. That he does it reluctantly. No man ever accuses himself of not loving his wife, above all in the conjugal act; of doing it to satisfy his needs, whereas it is an act of love. Your religious life is the will of God on you. What is the will of God on you? That you love your husband, your wife, your children, and your work, and that you show your love of God therein. And if you find that it is not going well, I will tell you to nourish yourself more, of course. You have to be more sacralized. You have to make the love of God enter into you more. You have to participate more in the love of God through sacraments and prayer: all of these are the means. But the essential is nonetheless there where you live and not where you eat. Your life is not spent at table. You have no more respect for God than you have respect for your life. And if you find that you have a stupid life then you have a stupid God.

Married people often tell me, "Oh, it's no use, I can't live a religious life! Ah! when I was young I went to Mass every day. I prayed, I went to days of recollection and retreats. Now I feel banished from all this—excluded, exiled! But when I'm a widow, when I'm retired, then I will finally be able to . . . But now I'm up to my neck in other things."

And I say, "I hope you *are* busy with your pots and pans! The worst thing would be to go to church instead of cleaning them. But do you clean your pots and pans with love? The whole problem is there."

When you go to Mass you say to God, "It is truly right and just, proper and helpful towards salvation, that we always and everywhere give thanks to you . . ."

And then you go back sadly to your stupid life, to your stupid cooking, to your stupid laundry, to your stupid factory, to your stupid office, where you are going to live your stupid life saying, "Ah! it is terrible to fall back into other things."

"It is truly right and just, proper and helpful towards salvation, that we *always* and *everywhere* give thanks to you . . ."

Is there anyone who has already prayed and given thanks where you work? Is there anyone who loves his work? Is there anyone among you who has already given thanks to God for the wife he has given him? for the husband he has entrusted to her? for the children he has given her? for the work he has put into his hands? Do you thank God for the mission he has given you? Do you give thanks? This is the Incarnation! It is one aspect of the Incarnation, and this is the spirituality for laymen.

For years I have tried to obtain from all the people I know a promise to pray a quarter of an hour each day. In the beginning I used to say half an hour! And for twenty years I have not obtained it, from the best people, not once. No one prays! Do not be surprised, your case is universal!

All the same, after twenty years, one begins to ponder. And this is what I have understood: deep down inside, what kept all these people from praying is that prayer was for them a source of remorse in their life. They had the impression that the whole of their life, the essential of their life, was profane, thoroughly profane, and that they were merely trying to clip off, on the side, a few minutes to devote to God. There was complete heterogeneity between their life and prayer. They would say a prayer and then fall back into material things. But deep down inside themselves they felt caught, held, absorbed, naturalized into the profane, and they finally dropped the superfluity, the remorse, the marginal activity: prayer. They felt ill at ease while praying, deserters of their true homeland, the world. And they felt foreign in the Church. They were the true "damned of religion."

The first prayer lay people should make is a prayer of thanksgiving. A cry of pride and joy! You should not be the pagans of the Church, the damned of the Church, but you should cry out with pride and joy: "Lord, I thank you for having entrusted this man to me. You trusted me, you could have put him in a monastery (he pretends from time to time that he would have enjoyed it!). But if you have entrusted him to me, it is, after all, the sign that you thought I would be capable of doing a better job than you. If not, you would have taken him for yourself. You have put this work into my hands, you could have taken care of it yourself, this task, this position, these parents, these children, this job. I thank you for having confidence in me, I am proud to do the job in your place, and I believe that you will give me all that I need to do it well, because it is not I who have chosen it, it is you who have chosen me, it is you who have sent me, it is your will which I accomplish."

I think that this is the first prayer, it is thanksgiving, which means "Eucharist." You come to Mass not to ask for grace, but to give thanks.

IV

How does one pray? What is it to pray?

The whole of Christianity is a participation in the death and Resurrection of Christ. Each sacrament commits us, associates us to the death and Resurrection. At your baptism, you were drowned like a little cat, and then you emerged, streaming with lustral water, renewed, washed, all new: dead and resurrected.

A confession, a true confession, is a death and a resurrection. Those who truly confess know this very well. A death to one's desires and a resurrection to love, grace, joy, the forgiveness of Christ which goes so far that we forgive ourselves for having sinned.

A true Mass is a participation in the death and resurrection of Christ. We say to God, "I don't want this day, I give it to you. I could eat my bread by myself, but it would not nourish me, I give it to you. And my life? I offer it to you. I have no confidence in my bread to nourish me, I have no confidence in myself to live my day, or to do my work, or to live my life. So here they are, take them." And God accepts them, receives them, consecrates them, sanctifies them, transforms them, transubstantiates them. He gives us his own bread, his own life, and he comes to live my day in me. Then, I can try to begin living. But not before dying and being resurrected.

Well, prayer is the great way of dying and the great way of being resurrected.

"There is a kind of devil which cannot be driven out by anything but prayer," Christ says.

What is your devil? Have you already put your finger on him? Do you feel him? He is at work! Your devil is your impulsive, violent, aggressive, closed, selfish, miserly character. Your way of being knotted up in yourself. There is a kind of devil which nothing can drive out but prayer. There is a kind of death that you can experience only in prayer. There is a way of dying to yourself which can take place only in prayer. Prayer is a participation in the death and resurrection of Christ.

If you read the Gospel, you will see this extraordinary thing: that Jesus always begins by refusing the prayers addressed to him. He always begins by making those who ask him die. Even the Virgin Mary: she began by asking the wrong thing. She met with a refusal. So she had to be totally confident: "Do whatever he tells you." She was heard.

Martha and Mary, the sisters of Lazarus, sent Jesus such a delicate and confident message: "Lord, he whom you love is ill."

Do *you* pray in this way? Do you have in your heart a certain number of "words of God," which lead you into a state of prayer? Most Christians have never taken the trouble to seek, to learn in which conditions they should place themselves to pray. So when they try, they yawn out of emptiness. And they justify themselves for never praying by saying, "I don't know how." Well, try! Say, "Lord, he whom you love, she whom you love is ill, very ill." Or the prayer of the Virgin Mary at Cana: "Lord, they have no more wine."

The miracle of Cana was the miracle of marriage, which means that even in marriage one has to die and be resurrected. There are two loves in marriage. The first is of flesh and blood: it has to die and a new love must then rise which is as different from the first as the second wine was better than the first. The second love of marriage is better than the first. But there is a death to experience, even in marriage, and a resurrection, because it is a sacrament. The wedding at

Cana is this: two delighted, enthusiastic, young married people have invited the Lord to their wedding banquet. It is not sure that they paid much attention to him, because they were very busy. But even so, the Lord was there. And then, as usual, a catastrophe happens: there is no more wine. A feast which ends up with water, a marriage which threatens to go adrift. The first conjugal disillusion. The first trial of life together. The first disappointment. The first failure. But the Lord is there. Very discreetly he is informed, he takes pity, he acts, he gives an order. And the second wine is better than the first. There is no true marriage before a death and a resurrection. But the second love is better than the first.

The official of the King "begged him to come down and heal his son" (John 4, 47). Jesus answers, "Unless you see signs and wonders you will not believe." Then this good man says, "Sir, come down before my child dies." He does not even discuss, he only implores. Christ looks at him and says, "Go, your son will live." Understand that for this man these words were a refusal, he had heard that Jesus would heal through contact, and he wanted to take Christ along, to bring him with him, to have him touch his son. He was sure that in this way his son would be healed. And Jesus tells him, "I will not come, you must believe, go." So the man stood there, gaping, tottering. Something was asked of him which was beyond his strength. "Should I insist? Should I go? But perhaps I am losing the chance of my life. I am going to go home, my wife will be there, and she is going to say, 'And the prophet—did you see him?' 'Yes.' 'And you did not bring him back with you?' 'No, he did not want to come.' 'Well, your son is dead.'" Then, according to the Gospel, he did not say a word, he was consumed. Christ has asked him what cost him the most. It is always exactly that which he asks: what one does not want to give. He left without a word, without thanks, absorbed in his effort of faith.

But the day after, when his servants come to tell him, "Your son is living," he only has one word: "At what time?" "Yesterday at the seventh hour the fever left him." And the man recognized that it was the time when Jesus had told him, "Go, your son will live." And he believed . . . He wanted to get hold of Jesus for a miracle, to extort a grace from him, and Jesus demanded of him a total confidence, demanded that he completely open himself to him.

This is the kind of death and resurrection one goes through in prayer. We die to what we were asking for, we are resurrected to him whom we were addressing.

To pray is to die. To die in an entire zone of ourselves, in which we are all too alive: agitation, pride, fear, resentment. And it takes a long time to die, and it hurts to die.

And it is to be born again in a zone of ourself where we are all too dead, and it hurts to be born.

The air which for the first time tears little lungs makes newborn babies cry. The life which comes back into a numb limb, the warmth which penetrates a frozen limb, makes us yell with pain! But it is the pain of being born. It is very painful to pray.

Christ took a whole night to say one sentence of the "Our Father," and we swallow the whole of it in a single gulp. But under cover of a Christian prayer we have kept our pagan mentality alive. We have to die to ourself to accept that his will be done and not ours. And if, for the Lord, this took a whole night, how long will it take for us?

This is why the sacraments are so ineffective. They no longer have any human context. They are so opaque and abbreviated that they no longer predispose to the grace which they communicate.

There is thus a fundamental contradiction between the effect proper to the sacrament and the disposition which someone brings to it. It is useless to distribute sacraments to people who do not pray, who do not want to pray, who do not want to die, who want only one thing: to remain themselves, in spite of everything.

The sacraments ought to be celebrated in such an authentic, expressive, and living way that it would be impossible to participate in them without feeling this obligation to die, and this call to be resurrected.

To die and to be resurrected takes time. God needs time! God has, in your life, in your esteem, the place he has in your time. You, too, say that you have no time to pray, do you not?

If you have no time for God, it means that you have no

esteem for him. You have time for everything that you consider important: your newspaper, your meals, your shower, and what not. If you have no time for God, it means that he has no importance for you. Practically, without prayer, you are an atheist, you who are sacred—the only sacred thing!

VII

The New Age of Hope

I

St. Peter says to us: "Always be prepared to account for the hope that is in you" (1 Peter 3, 15). What is your hope?

A few generous Christians hope for the whole Church to be in a state of mission, of poverty, but the great majority of Christians hope only that the hope of the others will not be realized!

Do you hope to go to heaven, for example? Do you hope for heaven, do you look forward to it? Do you await the resurrection of the dead? Do you desire it? An eternal life! But who wants it? We are in no hurry.

But do you have anything which can be made eternal? Have you savored anything good enough to wish it to be eternal? Do you love anyone enough to want to live with him or her forever? Are there moments of your life which you wish to immortalize? This is the whole question. Do you love the world, things, enough to want to make them participate in your own eternity?

Heaven is in close continuity with earth. The dogma of the resurrection of the body means that celestial happiness will be a human happiness. Heaven will be to your taste if you have good taste; it will resemble the best that you have experienced on earth. If you have nothing to immortalize, what will you fill your eternity with? I know only one Christian morality: begin a life good enough to want to live it forever. Do things which you will want to do for all your eternity. Do not await a life to come: it is the summit of idealism of the worst kind. There is no future life . . . there is only an eternal life, and it is "to know thee, the only true God, and him whom thou has sent, the God made man, the man-God."

The question is this: does Christ leave us on earth in order for us to demonstrate our good will until he sets us free from this world by introducing us into his heaven? Or has he given to the world natural and supernatural forces capable of transforming it little by little, of making it a place where justice dwells and where people love one another?

In the whole history of the world, one sees that salvation has always been indivisibly the work of God and of man. Creation: God found someone who would take care of the rest.

There is in our time a terrible crisis of hope. Why? Precisely because we are beginning to understand that it is possible for the world to commit suicide. Because problems have become terribly complicated. Because the individual feels so hopelessly powerless.

But for the time being, man can have the minimum well-being necessary if he is to practice virtue. In fact, for the first time in the history of man we are beginning to see that an evangelization of the world is possible. And we are beginning to see what the evangelization of the world would be like: that the word of God be announced to each people in its own language, its own culture, its own structures. And we can see that it is an immense, infinite task which, it seems, had never been thought of.

We are the first Christians! On the scale of the evolution of the world, two thousand years are nothing. This does not mean that nothing has been done before us. It means that a great deal has been done to put us where we are today! We are beginning to see the breadth of the problems, but we are also beginning to see that they can be solved. We have the date of the end of the world. It is given in St. Matthew: "When this Gospel of the kingdom has been validly preached throughout the whole world, then the end will come." We now realize that it is going to take a long time. A true announcement of the Gospel, of the good news, will be made not through imperialism, not through spiritual colonialism, but through proclamation. The Gospel does not say that the world must be converted, only that the world must hear the word of God.

When the Gospel is validly announced to each nation, the world will end.

What hell have you shut yourself up in recently? Do you

not remember? You shut yourself up in the hell of your intellectualistic, individualistic, idealistic paradise instead of beatifying yourself in the love of your brothers.

Hell is the expression of God's respect for our freedom. He is so respectful of our freedom that he will respect it eternally.

Are there many people in hell? No one knows. The Church has canonized saints. She says that there are saints in heaven, but she does not damn anyone. She has never said that someone was in hell!

Every time you go to Mass you pray "for our salvation and that of the whole world." Well, what is the object of prayer is, after all, the object of hope. The Church gives us the right to hope for the same thing which she gives us the duty to pray for!

II

I believe that we have to account to the world for our hope! The world suffers from a terrible crisis of hope. It is Teilhard de Chardin who said, "The world will belong to whoever offers it, already on this earth, the greatest hope." What is the hope that you propose to the world?

I will sum up the theme of this whole book by saying: you can give hope to the world, providing that you announce not an individual salvation, but a fraternal redemp-

tion: the full number of the Gentiles and the Jews along with us. We are responsible for one another, and we want to save everyone.

An individual salvation is something intolerable for a modern person. Péguy has rightly said, "The city which closes its doors to a single person is an unjust city which I do not want to enter."

Do you not need everyone to be saved? It is the only motive for which it is worthwhile to go to Church, worthwhile to love one's neighbors, worthwhile to consecrate one's life, worthwhile to enter a convent.

You should not aim at less than saving the entire world! Always be prepared to account for the hope which is in you! Christ's death was the "desolating sacrilege" which St. Matthew speaks of: the body of Christ, the true temple, was profaned, unveiled, and this sacrilege justifies the words of Jesus to the women of Jerusalem: "Weep for yourselves and for your children." Can you imagine any other crime "such as has not been from the beginning of the world until now and never will be?" Compared to this, what is the destruction in the year 70 of the Temple of Jerusalem?

The worst is thus behind us. The most terrible event of the history of the world is past. And it is lack of intelligence and faith to still expect it and be afraid of it.

Nowadays we are in the glorious phase of the kingdom of God, in a time full of joy and hope: the risen Christ, as he predicted, is sending his "angels," which means his messengers, his missionaries, that is to say, you, to gather to-

gether his elect from one end of the world to the other. It is the time of the Church, the time of the irresistible expansion of the mission of Christ.

If Christianity has spread first in our western civilization, with such a luxury of material development, is it not in order that we supply the whole earth, along with an authentic evangelization, that minimum of food and joy with which the millions of men presently underfed and exploited will be able to give homage and thanks to God.

It is so good to think that the world will end the day we have shared our bread so well that all peoples will be able to offer it!

"It is ever through him that all good gifts, created by you, O Lord, are by you sanctified, endowed with life, blessed, and bestowed upon us"—the entire world ought to be able to say this, thanks to you. For once, sharing the bread of Christ would have taught Christians to share theirs; they would have supplied the funds for this world-Eucharist. Christ would have become living enough again in them to renew the gesture by which he is recognized: "They recognized him in the breaking of the bread." And in an immense acclamation of joy, the world would rise towards God proclaiming, "Through him, with him, and in him all honor and glory is given to you, God, almighty Father, in the unity of the Holy Spirit, for ever and ever."